SCRAPBOOK *workshop*

The Best Techniques From Your Favorite Scrapbook Bloggers

Edited by May Flaum

MEMORY MAKERS
Cincinnati, Ohio
MemoryMakersMagazine.com

Contents

Introduction

So many crafters blog, and over the last few years blogs have become a part of my daily reading routine and creative inspiration. I love that I can be inspired, see craft projects, learn techniques and get my creativity going thanks to the fabulous individuals who share their ideas, work and creative process online every week. In addition to getting new ideas, I've gotten to know the crafters better through their posts.

In this book, I am thrilled to bring you a collection of techniques and projects from some of the best paper-crafting bloggers. Not only do these ladies blog regularly, but they are tremendously talented and share a wealth of knowledge as well as personal stories and tidbits of their lives through their sites.

It is my pleasure to lead this team of crafters. From digital brushes to fussy cutting paper, inked and distressed projects to floral embellishments, the collection of ideas in this book is as diverse as the contributors. Not only will you be inspired by new ideas and techniques, but you will also have these crafters' website addresses so you can visit their blogs and find even more.

Whether you are new to scrapbooking or an experienced crafter, I hope you enjoy *Scrapbook Workshop*.

May

Anna Aspnes is a digital scrapbooking artist, designer and instructor best known for her use of brushes and her artsy blended style. I enjoy visiting her blog to see what products she's been creating and how she's using them, and, in general, for digital inspiration. Her approach is artistic, and I always leave her blog feeling inspired and encouraged, never overwhelmed. I really like the glimpses into her creative process, seeing all that she does with digital products. I also appreciate the peeks at products she's releasing and classes she is teaching.

Anna is a British-born, U.S. Air Force wife living in Colorado with her husband and two children. She loves to push the realms of digital and create outside the box well into the night.

You

This layout celebrates a single chance shot of my husband and son during Christmas 2010. I made the photo large in spite of the technical imperfections because it portrays the tender side of a relationship between father and son. I create single photo layouts less often than I do a layout with multiple photos. So, I used the cast shadow technique to add interest to an otherwise flat and simple page.

Supplies: Adobe Photoshop; ArtPlay Palette Weihnachtsbaum-Anna Aspnes, Little Bit of Messy Love WordART-Ali Edwards (www.designerdigitals.com); font-Pea Kadee

Realistic Drop or "Cast" Shadows

The drop shadow is a layer style in Adobe Photoshop and Adobe Photoshop Elements that allows the scrapbooker to add a level of realism to any digital element in either a fully digital or hybrid project. The *Drop Shadow Layer Style* provides the illusion of depth to a physically flat page, mimicking the dimensional layering found in paper scrapbook pages. The default *Drop Shadow Layer Style* applies a uniform shadow to any element, but this shadow can be separated from the element and then warped to create a cast shadow, which provides an uneven—and therefore more realistic—appearance.

MATERIALS

Adobe Photoshop

ArtPlay Palette
Weihnachtsbaum-Anna Aspnes
(www.designerdigitals.com)

Little Bit of Messy Love WordART-
Ali Edwards
(www.designerdigitals.com)

Font (Pea Kadee)

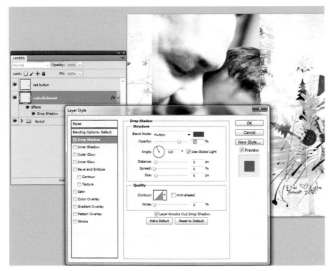

1 Create a digital layout with photos, papers, digital brushes and embellishments. I have grouped some of the layers in the *Layers* palette, excluding the embellishments.

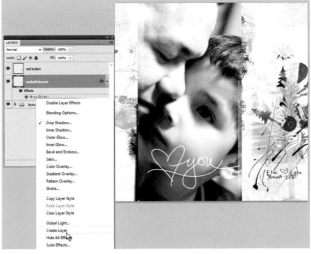

2 Select one of your embellishment layers in the *Layers* palette and apply a *Drop Shadow Layer Style* to that layer. Click on *Layer* in the *Options* bar at the top of the screen and select *Layer Style,* followed by *Drop Shadow,* from the fly-out menus. Notice the *fx* symbol and the drop shadow effect attached to the embellishment layer in the *Layers* palette.

3 Mouse over the drop shadow label in the *Layers* palette and right click (or *Control* click) to activate a fly-out menu of options. Select *Create Layer* from the menu. A dialogue box will appear stating that *"Some aspects of the Effect cannot be reproduced with layers!"* Click *OK.* The same result can also be achieved by duplicating the embellishment layer, converting the original layer to dark gray and then applying a slight *Gaussian Blur Filter* to the layer. Notice that the drop shadow layer is now a separate layer beneath the embellishment layer and that there are two layers.

4 Select the embellishment's drop shadow layer in the *Layers* palette and apply the *Warp* tool. Click on *Edit* in the *Options* bar, select *Transform* and then *Warp* from the fly-out menus. Notice the grid that appears around the embellishment. Drag the handles of the grid outwards to warp the embellishment's drop shadow layer. Double click on the grid to accept the transformation.

5 *Optional*: Apply a *Gaussian Blur Filter* to soften the embellishment's drop shadow layer. Click on *Filters* in the *Options* bar, select *Blur* and then *Gaussian Blur* from the fly-out menus. Adjust the lever in the dialogue box to increase/decrease the extent of the blur. *Note: You can also adjust the opacity of the layer in the* Layers *palette to lighten a shadow or create a shadow that is less harsh in appearance.*

6 Repeat Steps 1 through 5 using the remaining embellishments to complete the layout.

Tip

. . . .

The drop shadow technique is easy to replicate, is very effective in its execution and is therefore appealing to both the digital and hybrid scrapbooker. Cast shadows can be applied to elements, such as titles, embellishments, photos and paper edges, to create that much-sought-after realistic "lifted" look easily obtained in paper scrapbooking.

Siblings

This layout combines the best of digital and dimensional paper techniques. I used the cast shadow technique to build depth and create separation between the three stacked photos supporting the blending focal image. I love using vibrant color in my scrapbook pages, and this layout is indicative of that practice.

Supplies: Adobe Photoshop; ArtsyBlendz-Squash Paperie, Squash Elements- flower, button, naked tape, family word transfers no. 1, brush set-ArtPlay Palette Barren Sunrise, Stitched -Anna White, Circle LoopDaLoops No. 1, Abstract FotoBlendz No.3, Chalked, Scribbled Hearts-Lynn Grieveson (www. designerdigitals.com); fonts-Jellyka Saint Andrew's Queen, Arial

Art As Life

DEBEE RUIZ *www.debeecampos.blogspot.com*

Inspire Lovely is the name of Debee Ruiz's Etsy shop, and I also think it's a perfect way to describe her and her blog. Filled with lovely images and breathtaking projects, I truly enjoy visiting her blog. I am always struck by her passion for great photography and her intense and wonderful way with detail and color in her craft projects. She has such a talent for color and being bold in her art. I love how she embraces her mess and approaches her craft with a no-rules, fun attitude.

Debee is an art lover, married to her favorite person in the world, Mr. Handsome. She loves making art in her sunny San Diego studio and enjoys spray painting anything she can get her hands on. Some things that Debee loves include banana cream pie, pretty paper garlands, lovely peonies, crazy sewing lines and Starbucks Frappuccinos.

Lovely Layers

Layers can be so much fun! In fact, I layer thrifted tea plates and cups around my studio and home for added inspiration. I *love* the visual appeal—the different floral and decor designs together are so stunning. Layering my tea plates and cups also applies to my love for paper.

I have so many scraps of paper and have found a unique and lovely idea to create something with them. Having all these little pieces gathered together in a collection is best. I often use pieces I've collected from old envelopes, leftover scraps of fabric and even some IKEA paper rulers! I'm going to show you how to put those pretty little pieces of paper together in a lovely way.

MATERIALS

Chipboard shape (Maya Road)

Vintage-inspired seam binding, glitter ribbon (Inspire Lovely Etsy)

Other: pencil, manila folder, scissors, vintage papers, gold sewing thread, sewing machine

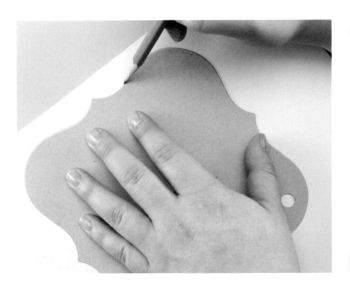

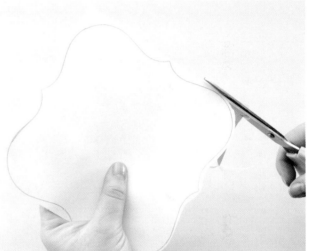

1 Trace a shape (any chipboard piece or shape will do) onto a piece of paper.

2 Cut around the shape. Do not cut too close to your lines and make sure to leave some white space around the edges of your shape.

« Hello Love XOXO

I've created a page using the lovely layer technique to add some style, texture and dimension to my page. I love the different colors and designs in the fabric, ribbon and paper combined. Of course, my favorite part is the collection of the pieces together. I have been hoarding some of these little bits and pieces for a while and love that even the tiniest piece stands out in this collection.

Supplies: chipboard shape (Maya Road); transparency frame, vintage-inspired seam binding, glitter ribbon (Inspire Lovely Etsy); anthropologie folder (Cavallini Papers & Co., Inc.); butterfly punch, mini butterfly punch (Martha Stewart, Marvy); pink ledger paper, mini crochet flower (created by me); Other: Manila folder, vintage doily, spotted feather, spray paint, vintage forget-me-not flowers, sequins, white carnival ticket, mini wooden clip, sewing thread, vintage papers

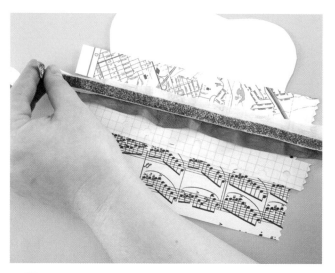

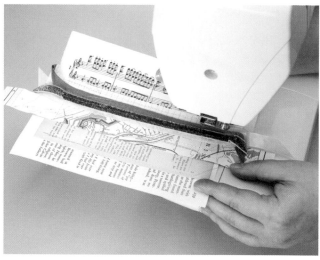

3 Flip the shape over so that the outline is on the bottom and the paper is facing up. Layer approximately seven pieces (or whatever number inspires you) of paper/fabric over your entire shape and cut strips of each piece longer than the width of your shape.

4 Glue or sew pieces onto the paper. *Note: It might be useful to quickly adhere some pieces with glue before sewing.*

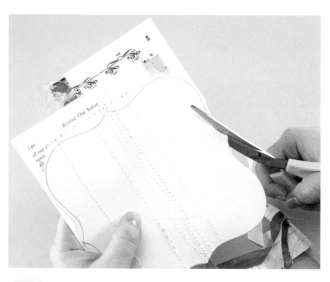

5 Once you glue or sew the pieces onto the shape, flip the shape over and cut along the traced lines. Then feel free to add adornments, paint splatters or anything that inspires you!

Tip

. . . .

Storing those precious bits of paper can be challenging. Try sorting the scraps by color and storing them in a file folder or in a series of drawers (depending on the size of your scrap collection). Then remember to turn there first for your projects.

My Inspiration

My inspirational color is black. You can never go wrong with black. I like how bold it looks, and it's definitely wonderful in a splatter form. Anytime I am making a lovely mess, I find it to be among my most inspiring moments. I allow myself the freedom to make mistakes and scribble stuff up; it's part of the artistic process. I embrace the mess. I find that to be the most inspiring aspect of several artists I admire. There are no rules, just a fun approach to art. I, too, want to be fearless in everything I do. No rules, just fun. I am constantly challenging myself to be dangerously brave, to get ridiculously crazy. No regrets, no right or wrong. Be bold! Break outside of my normal routine and really take joy in making an inspiring lovely mess.

XO Tag

I designed a little tag to go with gifts and tuck little notes in for my lovely family and friends. What makes it most rewarding is that even though it only took a few minutes, both my family and friends really cherish the one-of-a-kind items that I make for them. Often, they keep the tags on display around their homes and work areas just for added inspiration. It's so lovely to have the things I create so cherished.

Supplies: mini manila tags (Inspire Lovely Etsy); butterfly punch, mini butterfly punch (Martha Stewart, Marvy); Other: sewing thread, vintage papers, sequins, vintage doily, spray paint

A Soldier Girl's Thoughts SASHA HOLLOWAY

http://sassysasha.typepad.com

Sasha Holloway is an amazing photographer, gifted crafter, and as she puts it, "just a military girl living in a paper and glue world." Her blog is an eclectic mix of her craft projects, photos and personal posts. I'm never sure if I'm going to find inspiration, shopping picks, a personal note or a craft project from Sasha, and I love that! In all kinds of ways, she is inspiring. She writes candidly, with an uncensored honesty that is refreshing and very real. Her scrapbook style is full of bold colors and her projects offer thoughtful journaling, great use of embellishments and detail, and stunning photography.

Having recently retired after serving her country for over sixteen years, Sasha is living in England with her sons while her husband finishes his tour of duty. HotTamales candies are a number one sweet spot for her while crafting—she hides them in her room so no one else can eat them.

Hello Card

The technique I used is hand-stitching. I simply traced around some stickers that were in a color not coordinated with the card and hearts. I then punched holes and used a backstitch to sew in-and-out. I finished off the card with a white gel pen for added effect. I also raised the card using pop-up dots to give the hearts more dimension.

Supplies: patterned paper (October Afternoon); cardstock (Bazzill); red felt hearts (Craft for Occasions); thickers for letters (American Crafts); foam dots (American Crafts); butterfly punch (Martha Stewart); floss (DMC); white Signo pen (Uni-ball); Other: needle, gem

Hand-Stitched Titles

I have always loved embroidery, and Amy Tan inspired me a few years ago to stitch titles instead of using ordinary products. I have been hooked ever since. It is very easy to do and if you use just the right font, or even your own handwriting, it will turn out fabulous. All you need is a needle, some embroidery thread or floss, and paper, though having a paper piercing tool and something to pierce into of some kind is a great help, too.

MATERIALS

Chipboard letters

Pencil

Paper

Pushpin/paper piercer

Embroidery floss

Other: cork trivet

1 Trace the letters you need in pencil on the paper that you have chosen for the project.

2 Use a pushpin, paper piercer or other tiny hole-punching device and punch holes along the traced letters. It is always good to have something to pierce into, so I use cork trivets. When piercing, make sure to punch the holes evenly spaced and not too far apart for even stitching. Once you have punched all your holes, erase your pencil marks if you'd like.

« My *Hello Card*

I decided to go simple and focus on the stitching, using it as the primary element on this card. I finished the stitching and punched a hole in a piece of cardstock slightly smaller than the card. Then I placed it on foam squares and mounted it on the front. Adding a swirl of stitches, some pen work and a few other little details quickly produced a cute card that I can now send to a friend.

15

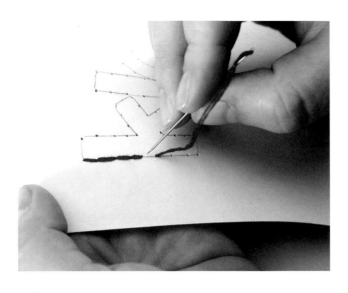

3 Using a needle and embroidery floss, split from 6 to 2 strings, and start hand-stitching using a backstitch technique.

4 Continue the backstitching until all the holes are filled. Then knot the floss and tape on the back.

Tips

* *This technique can be done with alphabet stickers, chipboard letters or even by printing a computer font in a pale gray.*

* *The fancier the font, the harder it will be to work with. Simple block style fonts are smart choices to start with.*

* *Besides letters, this can be a great technique to use on basic shapes, flourishes and in many other ways! Hand-stitched detail adds both visual interest and texture.*

* *Choose a color of thread that pops. Go for contrast between the thread and the paper you're stitching on.*

My Boys »

First, I did the title and worked around that. Since I was already working with a background, I wanted to keep things simple. Trace letters, punch holes and use a backstitch to complete. Instead of using 6–7 journal lines, use one big journal block as a focal point of the layout to keep the eyes from wandering. Using the Sew Easy tool, I made straight zigzag lines to keep it neat.

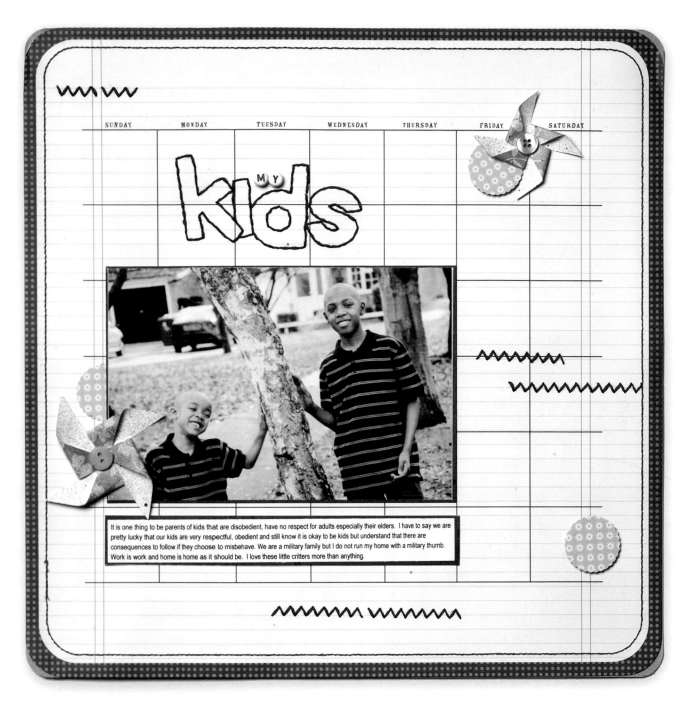

My Boys

I love this layout. By working with light blue and a bright contrasting red, it keeps the focus on my boys in this great photo. I hand-stitched the title using standard DMC floss. I love using pattern paper as my background, so this calendar paper was the perfect backdrop not only for my picture but the hand-stitched title as well, since it had stitching around the edge.

Supplies: patterned paper (October Afternoon); pattern paper calendar (KI Memories); cardstock (Bazzill); photo paper (Hewlett Packard); charcoal chalkboard mists (Tattered Angels); Sew Easy Stitch Piercer Zig Zag (We R Memory Keepers); circle cutter (Martha Stewart); corner rounder (EKSuccess Brands); floss (DMC); Other: buttons, letter beads

Balzer Designs   JULIE FEI-FAN BALZER   *www.balzerdesigns.typepad.com*

Julie Fei-Fan Balzer is a self-taught mixed-media artist and avid scrapbooker. She loves art that looks handmade—lots of painting, inking and wonky lines. She is also a technique-a-holic who is always trying to figure out new ways to use her craft supplies. When visiting her blog, you'll find an eclectic mix of projects—all of them with bold colors and hand-painted detail. She is a master at making simple paint and lines become something exquisite, and I am glad that I discovered her and her blog last year. Julie is an instructor as well as a designer, and her passion for her art comes through with each project and blog post. Always cheerful and inspiring, Julie's blog is a creative must-read.

Julie and her husband live in a two-bedroom apartment in New York City. They sleep in the "guest" bedroom because the master bedroom is her craft room. She creates with her two must-haves in easy reach: a glass of Diet Coke on one side and a heat gun on the other.

May

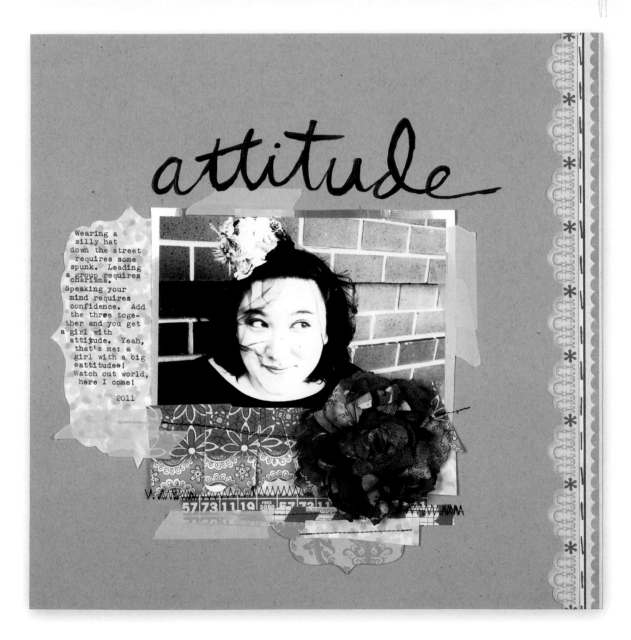

Hand-Painted Title

A hand-painted title adds movement and personality to a scrapbook page. No more searching for letter stickers that don't have the right letters or worrying about whether you've left enough room for the title—a hand-painted title is so flexible and easy to do. If you can write with a pen, you can hand-paint a title!

MATERIALS

Paper

Pencil

Brush

Black paint

Eraser

1 If you're nervous about jumping right in, sketch out your title using a pencil.

2 Paint the title, being sure to put as little pressure as possible on the tip of the brush. *Note: Be sure to keep redipping your paintbrush into the paint and/or water for a smooth line.*

« Attitude

I love to use bright colors! I love the warm and sunny feeling of this layout with the contrasting pops of turquoise. The strong black title at the top is echoed in the black hair, shirt and stitching on the layout. This layout embraces imperfection from the wonky painted title to the curving stitched line behind the flower.

Supplies: cardstock (Bazzill); Claudine Hellmuth Studio Paint (Ranger Ink); Koi Watercolor Paint (Sakura); paint, gesso (Golden Artist Colors, Inc.); patterned paper (Hambly Screen Prints); patterned paper (Sassafras Lass); stencil (The Crafter's Workshop); Tim Holtz Flower Die (Sizzix); Other: book pages, washi tape, machine stitching, typewriter

3   Let the paint dry and erase the pencil lines.

Tips

* *If you're not happy with your hand-drawn title, you can print (in a very light gray) your title in a size and font you do like and paint over it.*

* *Lose the pressure! Practice on scraps of paper until you are comfortable.*

* *To kick it up a few more notches, highlight with a second paint color, add glitter glue, pen work, or otherwise add more layers to your already great painted title.*

Working With Paint

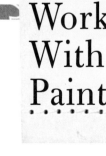

* *If you're new to working with paint, experiment a bit with the consistency of the paint and see what gives you the best results. Add a few drops of water to the paint to make it thinner. A thin, but creamy consistency might work best for this type of lettering.*

* *Experiment, too, with applying more or less pressure on the brush as you paint. Lifting the brush gradually as you paint results in a cool, tapered line.*

In the layout: hand-written journaling "He takes photos of everything—: food, quirky people, urban" and the large painted title "Shutterbug" with "texture, etc. Matthew has really become quite the shutterbug! 2011"

Shutterbug

On this project, I painted a similar title, but I also used simple lines and curves to create the patterned paper on the layout. I think the frisky painted line helps make the page feel fresh and full of life and movement. I love how the colors and one-of-a-kind accents I made make this a truly unique page. If you want to give this a go, just have fun! Relax and paint up a storm, then you can cut and use the pieces you like.

Supplies: cardstock (American Crafts); watercolor paper (Arches); gesso (Golden Artist Colors, Inc.); Koi Watercolor Paint (Sakura), Micron pen (Sakura); gold foil (Rubber Stamp Concepts)

Be Creative DEENA ZIEGLER *www.deenaziegler.typepad.com*

Not only does Deena Ziegler share projects frequently on her blog, but she also sells paper-crafting goodies and kits. She believes that being creative every day helps to stretch her imagination, and her commitment shows. Whether it's a cool photo, new card or other crafty project, Deena regularly posts on her blog and inspires her readers.

Deena is a mother of two and lives in southern California, where she just moved into a new craft room within her home. She loves designing cards and crafts, teaching and stumbling upon new techniques and ways to use old favorite products.

Forever Friends Scrapbook Page

For this project, I used one ink color applied to the embossed side of an embossing folder. I love the texture and interest this adds right next to the faces of my daughters.

Supplies: die cut machine, embossing folders, die cuts (Sizzix); cardstock (Core'dinations); patterned paper, embellishments (My Mind's Eye); trim (Making Memories); ink (Stampin' Up!)

Creating Colorful Dry Embossed Paper

I'm always looking for new ways to use my products, and I love the idea of being able to add the richness of ink, and depth of color to my embossing. With all the beautiful inks and embossing folders available, the possibilities seem endless. With any color, and any design, you can add endless looks to your projects.

MATERIALS

Die cut machine,
embossing folders, die cuts (Sizzix)

Cardstock (Core'dinations)

Ink (Stampin' Up!)

Other: brayer

1 Cut cardstock to the size of the embossing folder. Choose a pigment-based ink that will contrast in color. Roll the brayer onto the ink pad and coat the entire roller.

2 Roll ink onto the embossed side of the embossing folder (the depressed side). Re-ink the roller as necessary. Make sure the entire surface of the embossing folder is evenly inked. A good amount of ink is necessary for a higher contrast. If you want a more subtle effect, use less ink.

3 Place the cardstock into the embossing folder.

4   Insert the folder into the die cut/embossing machine.

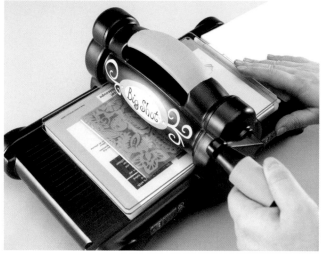

5   Roll the folder through the machine. You will hear the impressing on the paper. Just to be safe, roll the folder back and forth a few times.

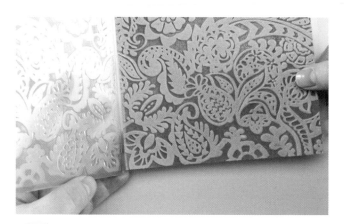

6   The cardstock will now be embossed with the ink on the debossed portion and the original colored cardstock will be embossed. The result is a beautiful two-tone embossed image.

More

For more possibilities, apply a second embossing and color layer to an embossed shape. Apply a second shade of ink, or in this case, use VersaMark ink. Roll the ink onto the embossing folder with the brayer. Then place the embossed shape into the folder and run it through your embossing machine for the second pattern. The result is a shape that is embossed with two different patterns. You can also highlight the second embossing with chalk to further reveal pattern.

May Your Day Be Blessed Card

Cards are just "my thing." I'm always on the lookout for ways to add texture and color. This card takes it a step further and shows a double embossing effect.

Supplies: die cut machine, embossing folders, die cuts (Sizzix); patterned paper (BasicGrey); ink (Stampin' Up!, Tsukineko) chalk (Pebbles); Other: ribbon

Tip
....

For this technique, choose an embossing folder that is a different pattern than your paper. If you choose an embossing folder with blank spots, wipe away any excess ink with a baby wipe after applying the ink (make sure the moisture dries before embossing). Also, using pigment ink will allow the ink to stay wet longer and give you more time to fully ink the folder.

Confessions of a Chocoholic MAY FLAUM

www.mayflaum.com

Brushed Titles

What I love about this technique is that it lets me go wild on my title work, and yet there is no mess to clean up because it's done in Adobe Photoshop Elements and the computer keeps it all nice and neat for me! By using the *Selection* tool and working with just my title letters, I can combine colors, shapes and looks for a unique stamped title that would be impossible to create with my paper supplies. The options are endless, and the technique is simple enough to enjoy no matter what your digital skill level.

Happy Moments

For this layout I used the *Brush* tool on the title and then mounted it onto a digital journaling element before printing it onto cream cardstock to use as the base of my layout. I love when my layouts mix paper and digital seamlessly, and the lines are blurred so it's not obvious which is real and which is printed from my computer.

Supplies: Adobe Photoshop Elements; patterned paper, tissue tape, sticker, staples (Tim Holtz); Adirondack mists (Ranger Ink); sparkler (Webster's Pages); painted journaler element-Katie Pertiet (www.designerdigitals.com); Other: buttons, thread, font- Broadway

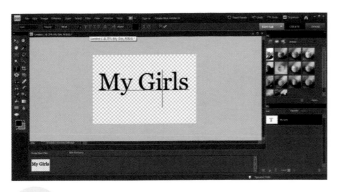

1 In Adobe Photoshop Elements, create a new blank file and type out your title text.

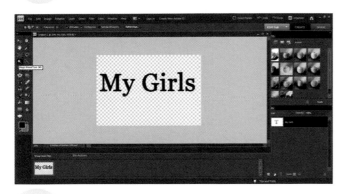

2 Click on the *Magic Wand* tool and select one of your letters.

3 In *Menu, Select > Similar* to select all of the letters. Now anything you do will only affect the letters.

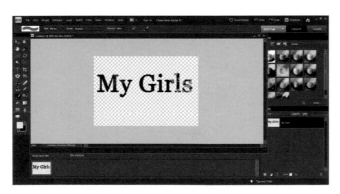

4 Select the *Brush* tool, and select the brush of your choice. Change the color to a contrasting color, adjust the opacity as desired and begin stamping your title.

5 Continue stamping until you are satisfied, adding different layers of color and different designs as desired. To finish, de-select the title and move this layer to your project or print it out at the desired size.

Tips

✻ *Thicker fonts will give you more space to show this effect.*

✻ *To add an outline to your letters go to* Edit > Stroke Outline Selection *and add the desired thickness and color.*

✻ *Use different brushes, colors and opacity levels to add more depth to your title.*

Brushed Title

31

I love how an oversized font becomes the centerpiece and my title thanks to the addition of some brushwork. I cut out the numbers and used a distress tool around the edges to rough them up before placing them in the center of my page. From there, all the other page accents and embellishments worked around that—and the page came together in a snap.

Supplies: Adobe Photoshop Elements; cardstock (Core'dinations); puffy pink (KI Memories); Distress Stickles (Ranger Ink); tissue tape (Tim Holtz); small letter stickers (Making Memories); digital butterfly brush-Katie Pertiet (www.designerdigitals.com); foam squares (Scrapbook Adhesives by 3L); Other: font-typewriter, thread, flower, button, lace

CONFESSIONS OF A CHOCOHOLIC

Paper Weaving

It's a simple technique, one that most of us were taught as children! Weaving paper back and forth, alternating and creating not just a pattern, but a sturdy surface as well, can be a lot of fun. What I like best about this is that I can change the sizes and tightness of weave, as well as many other factors, to create a completely one-of-a-kind background for my paper projects.

Love You

I wanted the "love you" part at the bottom of the page to stand out and not be interrupted by weaving, so I only wove about ¾ of this page. I like the effect it made by not going all the way to the left or bottom, and I think it helped me create a nice base for my photo. With weaving a funky mix of colors like this, I love how it lets me cut loose and add even more wild detail than I normally would. With some stitching, black dot rub-ons and plenty of little accents, I love how this page turned out.

Supplies: paper, number stickers (Echo Park); pink cardstock (Core'dinations); black dot rub-ons, pink alpha letters (Glitz Design); sparkler accents (Webster's Pages); butterfly punch (Martha Stewart); journaling paper (Jenni Bowlin); Other: thread, lace

Paper Weaving

1 Cut strips of paper. Also cut your background paper, but make sure to leave the last ½"– ¾"(1cm–2cm) attached so that it creates a fringe and better base.

2 Begin weaving paper. Alternate strips, and feel free to either leave space or create a tight weave, depending on your desired effect. Use a small amount of adhesive now and then to keep the finished pieces in place.

3 Once the weaving is complete, you can add mists, glitter, stamp and otherwise embellish the piece.

Tips
. . . .

✱ *Play with scraps, try mixing in ribbons and fibers, and change up the widths of your pieces. It does not have to be uniform.*

✱ *Mix and match colors and pattern sizes for either a more striking or more mellow-looking paper weave.*

✱ *Try die cutting or punching your finished piece to create unique embellishments. Just be sure you have used ample adhesive on each piece so it does not fall apart.*

We saved and planned for so many months, and our Disney World vacation was everything we hoped for. The 4 of us exploring the 4 parks and having a great time! ♡ 12/2010

4 Parks, 4 of Us

The variations for playing with woven paper are truly endless, and I wanted to try my hand at making an incomplete weave work for my layout. I cut some of the ends at an angle to better suit my design needs, and I used wider strips for the strips going across the page just to mix it up a bit more. What I really appreciate is how much this technique adds to my projects, without adding more time or expensive tools.

Supplies: patterned paper, brads, stickers, crepe paper embellishment (The Girls' Paperie); floral die cut (Tim Holtz); Other: craft cardstock, thread

CONFESSIONS OF A CHOCOHOLIC

Yeah Because

For this collage, I used three photos lined up in the middle and added a pink butterfly digital "stamp" behind them several times. Once printed, I added lots of texture and layers to bring together a simple page that focuses on my daughter and her favorite saying.

Supplies: Microsoft Word; patterned paper (Jenni Bowlin); cardstock (Core'dinations); ribbon (American Crafts); letter stickers (Doodlebug Design Inc.); sparklers (Webster's Pages); butterfly brush-Katie Pertiet (www.designerdigitals.com); Other: large flower, buttons

January Snapshots

I created a two-page Microsoft Word document and placed a total of six photos (sized 3"x4" [8cm–10cm]) across them, alternating so that once printed and trimmed, I would have this effect. I could have added rectangles of digital paper, but instead I added scraps into the spaces once printed. Adding a few sparkles, stickers and other fun elements made this two-page layout both a pleasure and a fast page to make. I love that I was able to get a bunch of recent snapshots onto the page that captures the girls' looks and outfits right now.

Supplies: Microsoft Word; letter stickers, rosettes, patterned paper, brads (The Girls' Paperie); sparkler accents (Webster's Pages); Other: thread, rhinestones, buttons

Collage in Microsoft Word

One of the most requested tutorials in my classes and most used techniques in my possession is to create a photo collage in Microsoft Word. Especially for scrapbookers who shy away from digital or don't have Adobe Photoshop Elements, it's a great way to ease into some hybrid scrapbooking without being overwhelmed. Using this familiar program, you can insert photos, add titles and text, and even add digital elements, such as papers and embellishments.

MATERIALS

Microsoft Word

1 Open a new Microsoft Word document. I generally prefer working in a landscape document. Go to *Insert > Picture > From File* and select the photo(s) you wish to bring into the document.

2 Change the orientation of each picture to *Tight* instead of *In Line with Text*. This will allow you to freely move your photos with no regard to the rules that would apply to text.

3 At this point, you can freely move your photos, and any cropping or resizing can be done at this time.

4 Once satisfied with the layout of your photos, you can insert a title using *Word Art*, journaling or other digital elements. To use *Word Art*, *Insert > Picture > Word Art*. Repeat Steps 2-4 if necessary, or simply print out as a photo collage and add elements to it later.

Tips

* *To change the order of images/elements, right click on the image and a menu will pop up allowing you to move it forward or backward in order.*

* *Changing all of the inserted elements (and any word art) to "tight" will let you move them freely without regard to the text rules. You can overlap, go to the edge of the page or anything else you please.*

Documenting My Days:
A Collection of Moments KATIE PERTIET

www.katiepertiet.typepad.com

She is a master of digital scrapbooking, creating both products and layouts. Katie Pertiet has been amazing me since I first discovered her work, and I've always loved reading her blog for both an insider's peek at her upcoming releases and the amazing projects she shares. She is the owner of www.designerdigitals.com, where she creates new products every week, as well as offers a wealth of information and inspiration for digital scrapbookers. She began designing products six years ago, and her style is very eclectic. Many of her products are my favorite digital items to work with in my hybrid crafting.

Katie calls Maryland home, where she lives with her family. Her favorite color is sage green and you can find that color all over her home and in florals all over her studio. While she loves munching on sweet treats, she tries to avoid eating while working. Of course, a cherry limeade is always welcome.

Mhm Good Stuff

In my sample, I used a light colored paper with some subtle creases. I also chose to blend the "good stuff" subtitle for added interest instead of the flat color. For that layer, I typed the words in a dark brown and used *Color Burn* as my layer blend mode, bringing out the textures of the neutral paper below.

Supplies: Adobe Photoshop; all items (www.designerdigitals.com)

Digital Blending

Blending is a technique that's really unique to digital scrapbooking. It's when your photos (or papers/elements) take on the attributes of the layer below them. I like to use it for adding texture and mood to my pages. It's great for fading photos. When you have a main focus photo and want to include an outtake, it adds depth to your page. *Color Burn* burns the colors of the upper layer with the lower layer. *Linear Burn* uses the darkness of the lower layer to mask the difference between upper and lower layers.

MATERIALS

Adobe Photoshop

All items
(www.designerdigitals.com)

1   After constructing your page, click on your photo layer so it is the active layer.

2   Adjust the blend mode for the layer. I chose *Linear Burn* for the sample page. After selecting, you'll notice your photo taking on the attributes of the layer below. Your choice of papers to blend with will affect your results, so some experimentation will be necessary to achieve a desired effect.

3   This is a screen shot after the *Linear Burn* has been selected and applied.

4 To blend other layers, simply select them and repeat the process.

"good stuff" **before using blend modes**

"good stuff" **after using blend modes**

Tips

. . . .

* *Remember to experiment with blend modes and layer opacity to refine your effects.*

* *Brushes blend too! Even alphabet stickers, buttons, photo frames and so much more! The possibilities are endless!*

* *Once you set your blend modes, you can change the color and saturation (Image>Adjust/Hue Saturation) of your paper to adjust the effects.*

* *Try the Screen mode for a lighter effect; it brightens by lightening the lower layer based on the lightness of the upper layer.*

* *Try the Overlay mode to multiply the light colors and screen the dark colors.*

Carefree

I wanted a very subtle effect on this photo. After clipping my photo (*Place the mask in the layer above the photo and choose Layer> Create Clipping Mask* from the *Menu* bar) to a decorative layer mask, I chose *Overlay* as my *Layer Blend* mode of the mask layer.

Supplies: Adobe Photoshop; all items (www.designerdigitals.com)

For the Love of Paper   KIMBERLY CRAWFORD

www.kimberly-crawford.blogspot.com

Kimberly Crawford shares so many lovely creations on her blog each week, and she always amazes me with how she takes a few items and places them together in a way that creates an awesome and striking project. Her inked edges, soft color palettes and love of cards are all things I've come to think of when looking at her projects. As someone who struggles with making cards, I find her blog a regular source of inspiration and a creative boost in finding new ways to use products.

Kimberly lives in Iowa, with her husband, son and cat. Aside from paper crafting, she enjoys golf, reading and playing the piano. Her favorite snack while crafting is Dark Chocolate Moose Munch.

Art of the Layered Strip

My style and layouts are very clean and simple, but I add interest by using this technique. It's an easy way to mix and match patterns by using a couple of simple tricks. By combining textures, sizes, patterns and colors, I can create a border or strip element that brings a detail and attention to my project. The best part is that I can use this technique on layouts, cards or whatever project I am creating.

MATERIALS

Paper

Cardstock (Papertrey Ink)

Ink

Ink applicator tool with pad

Other: adhesive, twine, ribbon-adhesive backed

1   Choose your papers, picking one with a small print, another with a medium print and finally one with a large print. Also choose papers with color contrast, to bring a little extra pop to your project.

2   Trim the papers to size, once again following the small, medium and large size idea. I inked the edges of my papers to bring a cohesive look to the different patterns.

« Snow

The border strip was not only the perfect location for the photos to rest, but also the title. The border has three patterned papers, a small print (the red snowflakes), medium print (black snowflakes) and large print (snowmen). The twine covers up the seam between the two papers. In this example, all the edges were inked to help provide a cohesive look. I added an extra border along the bottom of the snowman paper by stamping snowflakes along the edge with watermark ink.

Supplies: patterned paper, stickers (BasicGrey); cardstock (WorldWin); Distress Ink- black soot (Ranger Ink); VersaMark watermark (Tsuki-neko); black twine (Divine Twine); white pom-pom (Prima Marketing Inc.); stamp (Hero Arts); black burlap buttons (Nikki Sivils Scrapbooker); big scalloped border grand (Spellbinders Paper Arts)

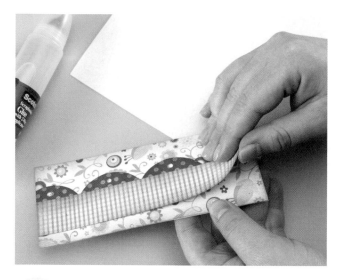

3 Adhere the paper layers together, but do not adhere the layers to your base yet.

4 Adhere your ribbon. Select color(s) that complement your papers, and also select varying widths and textures to add more interest to your project. I like to use twine to add a thin detail.

5 Adhere the entire piece to the base of your project.

Tips

* *Use this technique as a border embellishment.*

* *To make the selection easier, consider using papers from a coordinating line.*

* *Tying the twine around the project allows the back of your project to stay clean. This is especially important for cards.*

* *I like to use ribbon to cover up the seams, or lines, between two different pieces of paper.*

* *Using ribbon with adhesive on the back ensures for a straighter application.*

* *To help tie in the strip to your layout, add stitching, buttons and rhinestones, work your title into the design, and otherwise bring elements into the strip.*

Best Wishes

For this project, I layered several different trims together. Instead of mixing patterns, I mixed textures. When layering trims, the same basic idea applies: small, medium, large. However, this time it is about the thickness of the trims. Instead of stamping the sentiment in one place, I masked the sentiment off and stamped the smaller words onto a strip of cardstock. It tucked perfectly into one of the layers.

Supplies: letterbox trim, patterned paper (American Crafts); white flower trim, sequins (Hobby Lobby); cardstock (Papertrey Ink); stamps (Hero Arts); Memento Ink (Tsukineko)

Scraplifting

One of the wonderful parts of being a crafter is being inspired by and trying ideas inspired by other crafters. Whether it's a design idea, color scheme or technique, there are endless ways to get new ideas and expand your scrapbooking horizons. This book is filled not only with techniques to try, but also with beautiful projects that you can use as the fuel for a future project. I've done just that, and inspired by the contributors of this book, I have created three different projects.

Pretty Girl in Plaid

This layout was inspired by Lisa Truesdell's stitching and misting title technique (page 81) and her 24-7 layout (page 83) that was shown as an example of this technique. I placed a chipboard butterfly on my page, misted it, then cut around the top ⅔ to slide my paper and ribbon strips in underneath. I love the look and texture that adding the mist gives to this, and combined with letter stickers, stitching and bits of paper, I really see why this is a favorite technique! It's a quick way to add color, detail and fun to your page while making the most of your stash.

Supplies: cardstock (Core'dinations); patterned paper, brads (The Girls' Paperie); rub-on (Hambly Screen Prints); butterfly punch (Martha Stewart); small letters (Cosmo Cricket); yellow letters (Sassafras Lass); journaling tag (Elle's Studio); mist (Studio Calico); chipboard butterfly (Jenni Bowlin); Distress Stickles (Ranger Ink); Other: thread, ribbon

Blue & Green Tag

Next I decided to try out the technique shared by Debee Ruiz (page 10) for making lovely layers. I can definitely see this technique being wonderful in all kinds of shapes, but I wanted to try a basic tag first and see how it went. I love the results! I just started at the bottom and kept adding, and when finished, flipped it over and cut the excess off, then added some stitching and details like buttons. For my color inspiration, I started with a patterned paper that had a sour green and aqua and chose bits and pieces that worked well with that. What a fun way to use scraps!

Supplies: patterned paper- floral, aqua, black (Pink Paislee); patterned paper- green, text (The Girls' Paperie); trims (Webster's Pages); ribbon (May Arts); notion tissue flower (Studio Calico); Other: buttons, manila tag, thread

That's the wonderful thing about scraplifting and getting inspiration from other crafters: You can start with their idea, add your own twists or combine it with even more ideas to create something new and wonderful. Whether you take a general idea, or a very specific design of a project, have fun and don't be afraid to change things up to work for you.

Love Card

Tammy Tutterow has a very interesting technique (page 110) for making monochromatic backgrounds with canvas, distress ink and a stamp. I decided to try her technique on a chipboard heart. Once I was finished, I decided to take it in my own direction by adding silver foil tape around the edges and rhinestones, and using embossing powder on it to seal it. Once complete, I decided to make my heart the center of a card and added trim and hearts stamped on patterned paper—an idea I got from Nora Griffin (technique on page 57).

Supplies: canvas, foil tape, UTEE powder (Ranger Ink); Distress Ink, Stickles (Ranger Ink); stamps (Stampers Anonymous, Catslife Press); patterned paper (Studio Calico); cardstock (Core'dinations); blue flower (Making Memories); Other: chipboard heart, trim, rhinestones, thread

Debbie Hodge manages to be both innovative and approachable and is constantly surprising and impressing me with her work and website. With a constant stream of articles, ideas and practical approaches to getting more scrapbooked, Get it Scrapped! has something for every scrapbooker. She is a digital scrapbooker these days, but she has roots in traditional scrapbooking and occasionally dabbles in paper, as well. Her warm and welcoming attitude makes her an inspiration to all scrapbookers.

Debbie came to Seacoast, New Hampshire, over twenty years ago to get her M.B.A., and now lives there with her husband and two sons. She is an author and designer and runs her own website that offers classes for both digital and paper scrapbookers.

In Spring

I used several repetitions of a bird silhouette for the masking and two types of brushes: One has the look of spray paint and the other is a thicker "watery spot" brush. Three colors—yellow, pink and brown—are used for the brushwork. The masking here is done on a patterned paper canvas and is messier and less clear than that on "Crazy Ride" (page 47). Less of the background canvas is covered. Adding outline strokes and sequin eyes to the birds makes the shapes more understandable. To make the page's bottom border, I used a scalloped strip, but instead of brushing around the scallops as I did with the birds, I filled in the scallops.

Supplies: Adobe Photoshop CS3; 28 Days Later (Pea Shirley fonts); The following digital supplies are from designerdigitals.com: Anna Aspnes-Straight Line Stitched Orange, SprayPaint No 1, SprayPaint No 2 BrushSets. Jesse Edwards- Shapes Brushes, Stamps, Boys Toys Paper pack. Lynn Grieveson- Mapmaker Paper Pack, Worn Photo Edges, Hint At It #7 Brushes. Pattie Knox- Absolutely Acrylic Rainy Day. Michelle Martin- Just Linens #2. Katie Pertiet- Krafty Journal Spots, Inked Alphabet #3, Rimmed Framers, Blank Safety Tags Vintage, Krafty Cuts Botanical

Masking Journaling Spots with Digital Shapes and Brushes

While I'm a digital scrapbooker, I often try to get the look of paper on my pages. I'm inspired by many paper scrapbookers and art journalers. Lately, I've loved the effects folks are getting with spray inks and mists. I like layering, and I'm realizing that mist, paints and inks are layers that can add a lot to my pages. Right after taking a class with mixed-media artist Dina Wakley, I worked on emulating the look she was achieving with ink and stencils on my digital pages—especially to make homes for my journaling.

MATERIALS

Adobe Photoshop

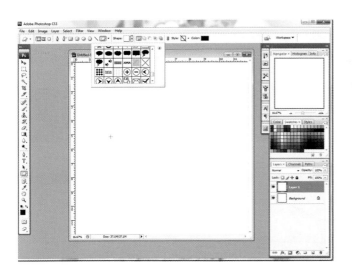

1 Open a new document. *File >New,* width=12" (30cm), height=12" (30cm), resolution =300 dpi, color mode = RGB color. Next, open a background cardstock and drag it onto your new canvas. *Note: You should use white or a lighter shade of the color that you'll be doing your brushwork on.* You can draw a shape, use one of the Photoshop shapes or any digital product for the journaling spots. To use an Adobe Photoshop shape, select the *Custom Shape* tool and use the drop down menu along the top bar to select the exact custom shape you'd like to use.

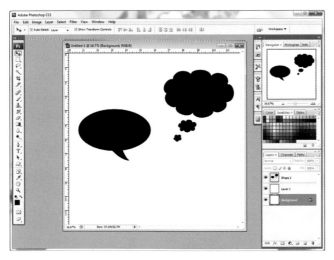

2 Draw or drag your shape onto your canvas on a new layer. Click on that layer. Set your colors to the Adobe Photoshop defaults of black foreground and white background, then drag out your shape. Use the *Select* tool to select your shape, resize and/or drag it to the position you'd like it in. Add as many talk bubbles or thought bubbles that are appropriate for your piece.

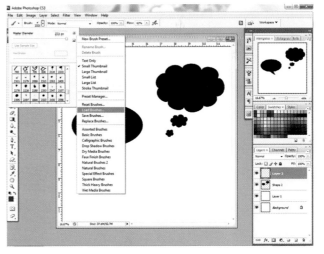

3 Select a color by double clicking on the foreground color box on the toolbar. If you do not like the default brushes, you can load new brushes into your window by selecting the *Brush* tool and then clicking on the dropdown for brush selection along the top menu. Select a brush shape. Set the *Flow* to less than 50% to begin with.

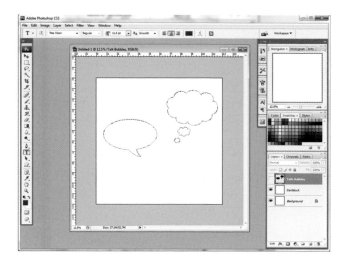

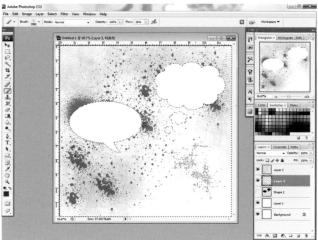

4 "Mask off" the area containing your shape so that your brushwork only "takes" on the areas outside of it. In the *Layers* palette, hover over the "thumbnail" for the layer holding your shape, then *Control + right click*. You will now see a moving line around your shape. Now press *Shift + Control + "I"*. Hide the shapes by clicking on the eye within the layer on the *Layers* palette.

5 With your *Brush* tool selected, paint! You can click once to paint one stroke. You can *Shift + cight click*, and drag to draw a series. You can press *Control + "Z"* to undo a stroke. Make new layers to hold different kinds of brush strokes. This way you can change color, opacity, blending modes or even delete later. Here, I used several of the *Spray Paint* brushes with the *Flow* set to 62%. I then added a layer below the strokes and used the *Hint At It* brushes at a much lower flow to fill in the background.

6 You can add definition to your shape with strokes/ outlines. Make a new layer to hold the outline strokes. Select the area filled by the shapes by press-ing *Control + right click* on the thumbnail for them in the *Layers* palette. Make the selection slightly smaller with *Select >Modify >Contract > 10 pixels*. Stroke the outline with the current foreground color with *Edit >Stroke >3 pixels*. Add journaling. You can either put in the journaling with forced returns and spacing to get it to fill your shape, or, if you have Adobe Photoshop CS, you can create a text path.

Tips
. . . .

✳ *Try different brushes and using multiple colors.*

✳ *Play with brush flow, shape and angle.*

✳ *Layer opacities.*

✳ *Play with beveling/embossing of your drips and splats.*

✳ *If your piece is staying digital, the RGB color mode is fine. If you are printing it, make sure to switch to the CMYK mode.*

Journaling (handwritten):

August, 2010. Oxford, NY. We should have known by the twinkle in his eye that Matt planned an out-of-the-ordinary hay ride for Mom's family reunion. We bumped & tipped & laughed like crazy.

Crazy Ride

The background canvas for this page was a very pale-blue textured cardstock. I used a digital brush of the sun as my mask and a darker blue color for my brushwork. I used spray paint, splatter and texture brushes to cover most of the background a deeper blue. The splatters are darker and run in an ascending diagonal path from the bottom left of the page to the top right. The brushwork and masked journaling spot are the first layers on this page and they create the foundation for it.

Supplies: Adobe Photoshop CS3; 28 Days Later (Pea Shirley fonts); The following digital supplies are from www.designerdigitals.com: Anna Aspnes- Straight Line Stitched Orange, SprayPaint No 1, SprayPaint No 2 BrushSets. Jesse Edwards- Shapes Brushes, Stamps, Boys Toys Paper pack. Lynn Grieveson- Mapmaker Paper Pack, Worn Photo Edges, Hint At It #7 Brushes. Pattie Knox- Absolutely Acrylic Rainy Day. Michelle Martin- Just Linens #2. Katie Pertiet- Krafty Journal Spots, Inked Alphabet #3, Rimmed Framers, Blank Safety Tags Vintage, Krafty Cuts Botanical

Gettin' By

LISA DICKINSON

Whether she's training for a marathon, sharing layouts from a recent craft session or writing about snippets from her daily routine, Lisa Dickinson never has a dull moment. I love how she shares her love of running, pretty things and, of course, scrapbooking through her blog. Lisa has a gift for coming up with the most fantastic ideas and designs on her pages, and turning mere scraps of paper into extraordinary creations. I'm always inspired to try more with inks and mists, and she never fails to give new design inspiration.

Lisa lives in Colorado with her husband and their children. She creates from her home office, where she finds inspiration from home decor magazines, children's books and various forms of advertising. When she's in a creative fury, you can almost always find her desk littered with scrap supplies, a Diet Coke and LÄRABAR wrappers.

Using an Acrylic Template to Create a 3-D Looking Element on a Page

Using spray ink, or misting, is all the rage on scrapbook pages these days! I love mist because it is so versatile and there's really no wrong way to use it. One of my favorite ways to use mist is combining it with an acrylic template (used as a mask) to make interesting, dimensional elements on the page. The spray ink adds a soft layer of color and when the template is removed, the unmisted background shows through. By filling in some of the shapes with patterned paper and outlining the edges with a pen, a unique dimensional effect results. And with the wide variety of templates and endless array of ink colors available to scrapbookers, you can make this technique look completely different on every page you create.

MATERIALS

Cardstock

Acrylic template
(The Crafter's Workshop)

Mist (Studio Calico)

Mark-It pen (BIC)

Patterned paper

Craft knife/cutting board

Other: twine, button, brads,
rhinestones

1 Use a temporary adhesive to lightly affix your acrylic template to the cardstock.

2 Holding the mist bottle about 8"(20cm) from your page, lightly mist over the template. Once your misting has dried, remove the template and clean it off using soap and water.

« Sparkle

This technique has major impact when you use a full page (12" × 12" [30cm-30cm]) template to create the background. I sprayed pink mist over the flower template and filled in a few of the flowers with patterned paper petals. The entire design is outlined with a light gray pen that adds subtle dimension. I topped it off with plenty of sparkle, such as rhinestones, glitter and pearlized buttons!

Supplies: cardstock (Bazzill); patterned paper, buttons, paint (Jenni Bowlin); acrylic template (The Crafter's Workshop); pink mist (Studio Calico); chipboard letters (Doodlebug Design Inc); rhinestones (Creative Charms); blue glitter (Sulyn Industries); Mark-It pen (BIC); font-American Typewriter

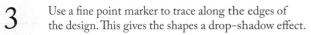

3 Use a fine point marker to trace along the edges of the design. This gives the shapes a drop-shadow effect.

4 Place your clean acrylic template over the patterned paper of your choice and trace several of the interior shapes onto it. Cut out the traced shapes and use them to fill in the centers of some of the areas.

5 Adhere your cutout shapes to the corresponding area on the design.

6 Adorn the design with various embellishments: buttons, brads, rhinestones or whatever inspires you!

Tips

* *It's better to apply several light coats than one heavy coat.*

* *Place the piece in a cardboard box to catch any overspray.*

* *Try with multiple colors of mists or color washes for different effects.*

Eat My Bubbles

On this layout, I used a white mist over a bubble/circle template. I filled in some of the interior spaces with glitter cardstock, patterned paper and brads in cool, watery tones. I love how the oversprayed mist and droplets play into the water/ swimming theme.

Supplies: cardstock (Core'dinations); acrylic template (The Crafter's Workshop); white mist (Studio Calico); patterned paper, glitter, cardstock, small blue brads (KI Memories); vellum (DMD Industries, Inc.); chipboard letters, rhinestone brads (Making Memories); pearlized brads (Creative Imaginations); blue felt brads (Imaginisce); rhinestones (Creative Charms); Mark-It pen (BIC); font-Traveling Typewriter

Kelly Purkey is quite possibly the most fabulous single girl in New York City. She enjoys filling up her life with wonderful friends, amazing adventures and travels, life in the big city, and lots of delicious food. Not only does Kelly keep a jet-setting travel schedule, but she's a scrapbooking rock star as well. Her designs are as fun and full of energy as Kelly herself. She shares projects and links to things she's working on frequently on her blog, as well as a variety of travel and food photos.

Kelly lives on the island of Manhattan in New York City, which is a dream come true for her. She works from home as a freelance scrapbooker and designer, but often flies around the country to teach classes or dip her toes in the ocean. Kelly loves photobooths, the Brooklyn Bridge, art museums, stamps in her passport and impromptu dance parties.

Misting Over Embossed Stamps

Using mists on layouts is such a hot technique, and I wanted to come up with a fun new way to use it. Combined with my huge collection of stamps, along with a little clear embossing powder, you ,too, can create a fun new look on your pages.

MATERIALS

Cardstock (American Crafts)

Stamps (Hero Arts)

Mists (Studio Calico)

Ink (Tsukineko, Stampin' Up!)

Embossing powder
(American Crafts)

Other: heat gun

1 Choose a stamp and ink with VersaMark or embossing ink. Stamp onto your paper.

2 Cover the stamped image with clear embossing powder.

« Happy Fall

Fall in New York is my favorite season, and I wanted the colors in the park to come through with the mists. I used the leaf stamps to create my own background paper, which I then misted with a few colors and mounted on brown cardstock. The leaf background, combined with stamping (and cutting out) leaves on cardstock was a fun way to match the photos. All that I needed to do once the stamping was finished was add a select few embellishments to bring it all together.

Supplies: cardstock, brads, embossing powder (American Crafts); stamps (Hero Arts); mists, labels, buttons (Studio Calico); letters (Making Memories); vellum (Paper Source); ink (Tsukineko, Stampin' Up!)

3 Shake off the excess powder and heat the stamp with an embossing gun.

4 Spray with color mists to desired color effect.

5 Wait until the mists dry, then wipe it off of the stamped image.

Tips
· · · · · · · · ·

✳ *Try this technique on a tag or as a small accent.*

✳ *Freehand doodle with glossy accents or other clear shiny medium and use that as a resist instead of a stamp.*

✳ *Try it with colored embossing powder.*

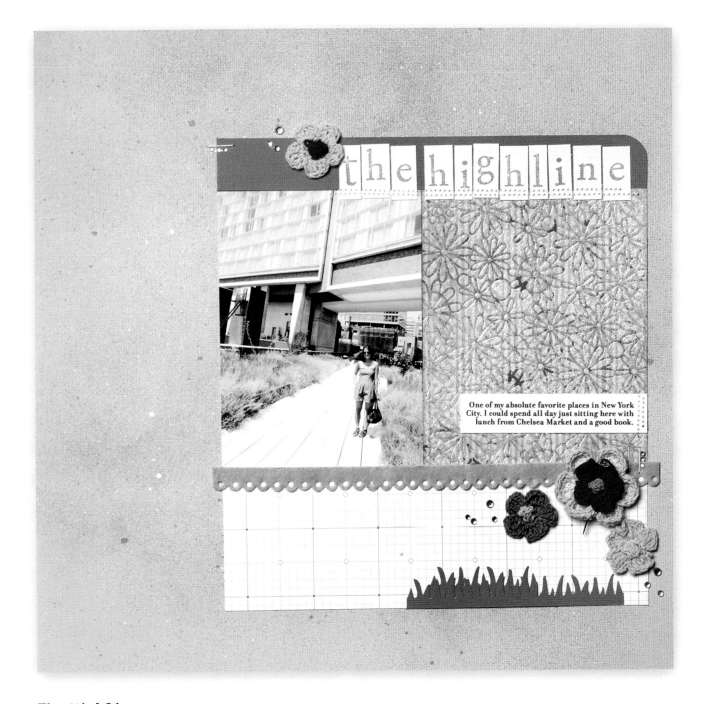

The Highline

I loved the blue-on-blue colors of the building in the photo and wanted to create a similar look with patterned paper and mist. I used a big stamp that was more of a solid pattern and stamped directly onto the patterned paper, then misted over the embossed image. From there, adding some other fun colors, textures and accents brought this page together, and I love the results!

Supplies: cardstock, flowers (American Crafts); stamps (Hero Arts); mists, patterned paper (Studio Calico); ink (Tsukineko, Stampin' Up!); gems (Hero Arts); paper punches (Fiskars); pin (Maya Road)

Nora Griffin describes her crafting style as full of lighthearted contradiction. Her blog is filled with details of her personal life as well as crafting projects, and she regularly shares interesting tidbits, lists and details. She is a firm believer that there are no rules in scrapbooking, and she embraces any crafting mistake as just needing to take a new direction. She loves patterned paper and stamping, and her creative yet approachable and very lift-able projects are always a welcome site on her blog.

Nora considers herself a lucky wife and mother, and calls southern California home. When she's not making stuff, it's because she is trying to be a responsible graduate student so that she can teach Sociology at the community college level in the next couple of years.

Brothers

For this layout, I incorporated stars onto a simple yellow pattern and carried it through with a little more stamping onto the punched stars. For the title, I layered stamping over graph patterns as opposed to simply using cardstock. Details like dimensional adhesive for the stars and roughing up the edges of the cardstock with a distresser help give the layout a little extra interest.

Supplies: patterned paper (The Girls' Paperie); star outline stamp, patterned paper (Studio Calico); patterned paper (American Crafts); patterned paper (Echo Park); star punches (Fiskars); paper distresser (Tim Holtz); star stamp (Stampers Anonymous); Name/Date stamp (Stampin' Up!); alphabet stamps (Educational Insights); small alphabet stamps (PSX design); ink pad (Jenni Bowlin, Clearsnap); Other: typewriter, graph paper

Stamping Over Patterns

I could call this "stampatterning," but that's a little cheesy, right? I have to admit, I am not one for lots of embellishments, but when it comes to rubber stamps and patterned paper, I can't get enough. That's how I ended up combining the two. If you keep an eye out for subtle background patterns, they can be made a little more fun by layering over them. It's a great way to bring other colors or images into your project.

MATERIALS

Large background stamp

Patterned papers

Office supply tag

Circle punch-2 sizes

Paper doily

Other: ink pads, scissors, foam tape, ribbons

1 Choose either a large background stamp or any design you'd like to repeatedly stamp to make a background on top of a subtle patterned paper.

2 Use an office supply tag as a template to cut down your stamped piece into a traditional shaped tag.

3 Use another subtle pattern (tiny polka dots are always fun) to stamp your birthday sentiment on top.

4 Since I used a circular stamp I punched it out for a little more definition.

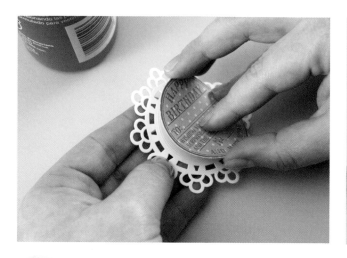

5   Other layers can be incorporated, especially when using pieces that have been stamped and cut out. In this case, I layered the birthday seal on top of a die-cut doily.

6   I use foam tape as an easy way to add dimension to many of my projects. It can be cut into pieces as large or tiny as needed.

7   When making tags, I try to include a fun reinforcement for the hole at the top. For this, I punched a small scalloped circle and used another smaller circular punch to make the hole both on the scallop and the tag itself.

8   No tag is complete without a tuft of cute ribbon tied to it.

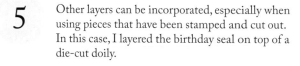

Tips

. . . .

✱ *Subtle patterned papers often work best for this. Ledger, dots, small print or light colors are great.*

✱ *When deciding on your ink color, keep contrast and your overall desired effect in mind.*

✱ *Use scraps of paper to test out different looks and to practice!*

Oakglen

I started with the simple graphic dot background and added the wood grain. One of the aspects of large background stamps that I try to embrace is the wonky imperfection that occurs when repeatedly stamping them. I like to think of it as character. To make the scallops, I simply stamped a stamp that shape onto red paisley paper and then cut out the stamp's outline to layer together a border. I used large alphabet stamps for the title right over the graphic dot background.

Supplies: patterned paper (BasicGrey, Anna Griffin); wood grain stamp (Studio Calico); "For the Record" stamp (Catslife Press); apple stamp (Paper Source); scallop text stamp (Stampers Anonymous); cardstock (Bazzill); alphabet stamps (Stampin' Up!); punches (EK Success Brands); ink pad (Clearsnap); Other: date stamp; graph paper

Life as a Three-Legged Dog BECKY OLSEN

lifeasathreeleggeddog.blogspot.com

Expect the unexpected, and be prepared for a good time is how I'd describe Becky Olsen. She has such a gift for layering elements, and her projects are always the kind I want to look at more closely. She comes up with amazing ideas, has a great way with words and has been working in the scrapbooking industry for quite a few years. "I am a lucky girl" is one of her mantras, and she keeps that happy spirit alive on her blog, sharing stories and plenty of craft projects.

Becky lives in Utah, where she is blessed to have a large room with big windows to the world to do her creating in. In fact, her blog is written while looking out those windows, often while birds are in the trees. She rarely snacks while crafting, but she sometimes sneaks dark chocolate chips from the pantry.

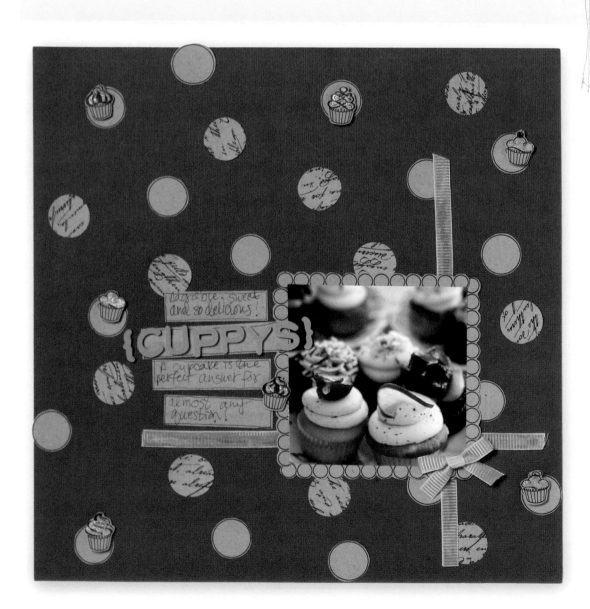

Fussy Cutting

Fussy cutting is a technique that has been around for a long time, where you use a cutting tool to separate an image from paper or cloth. It is one of my favorite techniques for adding texture and dimension to a page without getting messy. It is quiet and can be a great way to craft while spending time with your family while watching television or chatting. The easiest way to begin fussy cutting is by starting with basic shapes and then adding a little more difficulty as your comfort level increases. Apply dimensional adhesives to the pieces you are adding to your projects for even more visual impact.

MATERIALS

Sweet Cupcakes, Pen & Ink and Mod Circles paper
(Hambly Screen Prints)

Cotton Candy Stickles
(Ranger Ink)

Foam Squares (Scrapbook Adhesives by 3L)

Other: circle punch, scissors

1 Identify appropriate images to use. Start by cutting out the larger circles and cut a few more than you think you might need just in case. Trim around a few lines of the smaller circles to use as a frame for any pictures you will be using.

2 Then cut out the cupcakes.

« Cuppys

I love the sweet simplicity of this layout. The open, airy space really lets the picture be the focal point, but the dimension created by the little circles and cupcakes moves the eye around and keeps it interesting. The circles remind me of sprinkles, not an intended part of the initial design, but a delicious surprise to the eyes nonetheless.

Supplies: cardstock (Bazzill); paper: Sweet Cupcakes, Pen & Ink, Mod Circles (Hambly Screen Prints); Thickers (American Crafts); Cotton Candy Stickles (Ranger Ink); foam squares (Scrapbook Adhesives by 3L); Other: ribbon, adhesive runner

3 Put a little bit of pink Stickles on them to look like icing and set them aside to dry while working on the other parts of the layout.

4 Next punch out or cut out the complementary script paper, then adhere both types of circles to the cardstock to create your custom background.

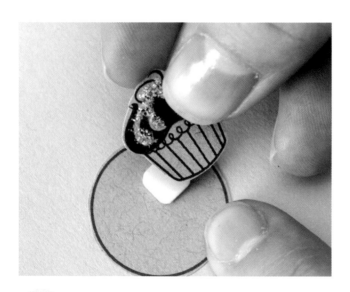

5 Use dimensional foam adhesive to adhere the cupcakes onto the circles.

Tips

. . . .

✳ *Always cut more than you think you will need; it will make the design process easier.*

✳ *When using fine tip scissors to cut, turn the paper, not the scissors; this makes for much cleaner cuts and your hand doesn't become fatigued.*

✳ *When I using a craft knife, make sure it is new and sharp. This makes for much cleaner cuts and is much less likely to create rips, pulls or shredding on the image.*

Floral Gift Bag

Getting a gift in a beautiful presentation is something that builds excitement and anticipation for me. Giving a gift that I have taken the time to beautifully create makes the moment that much sweeter when it gets handed over to an excited recipient. This gift bag looks like it took hours to create, but because the flowers are so big and beautiful, it was easy to cut out and really didn't take long at all. When selecting images for presentations like this, make sure to get a few sheets so you can double—or even triple—layer images for that extra pop of delightful dimension.

Supplies: Picture Perfect, Sweetest Day (Pink Paislee); Union Square "Home Sweet Home" (My Mind's Eye); Labels Two die (Spellbinders Paper Arts); Distress Ink- Old Paper, Antique Linen, Frayed Burlap (Ranger Ink); silk ribbon- Rose (May Arts); Other: gift bag

Live From Tormville Sharyn Tormanen

www.sharyntormanen.typepad.com

Sharyn Tormanen has been scrapbooking for most of her life and blogging for about six years now. Her blog is updated almost every day with tales from her daily life and the occasional scrapbook layout. While not a traditional craft-filled blog, it's something special, and a reading experience I treasure. Sharyn has such a way with words, knowing just how to tell stories of everyday life in a way that I can't look away, and that is an incredible gift. So often in her writings, I get ideas for future pages, things I should photograph, notes I want to make about my own life. I'll continue to read and enjoy it as long as she keeps writing. I love her classic scrapbook style and outlook on life in general.

Sharyn calls Michigan home, where she lives with her husband and four children. When scrapbooking, it's not unusual for her to begin with the story. She has a little corner in her kitchen where she stands and creates. She does her best to make time for the kids and time for herself each day. It's one of the reasons that having her craft area right in the kitchen works.

Sharyn's Scrappy Borders

I like this technique for several reasons. The first reason is it's a great way to use up scraps, and to use them in such a way that they really create an impact. I also like that it's an easy way to bring a lot of color to a layout without overpowering the story or the photos. Finally, I love this technique because it's so easy, but it looks like it's time-consuming. It's not. And, there's a multitude of ways to use this technique and bring it to life.

MATERIALS

Patterned papers

Chipboard/cardstock

Other: craft knife, ruler, cutting mat, adhesive

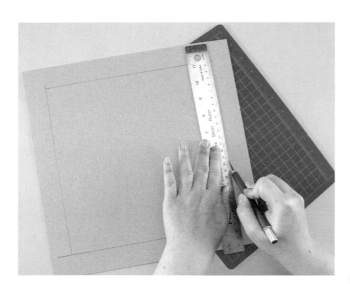

1 Decide first what to create your border on. Here, I used a thin piece of chipboard. (These are often included in scrapbook product orders, and I like to make use of them.) Cardstock is also an option. Then cut your border to shape.

Tip
· · · · · · · · · ·

When cutting chipboard, use a new blade and cut slowly. If you like, use the back of the blade to make a score line. Then make the final cut in the scored groove.

« And Now She is Nine

This technique could easily be applied to a straight border, a title or just an embellishment. In this layout, I used the technique to border the entire page. I love that I was able to keep it fun by bringing in a variety of colors, but at the same time not take away from the focus of the layout. To me, the layout screams fun and happy, just like the nine-year-old girl it's about.

Supplies: title stickers- Jack and Jill (Doodlebug Design Inc.); die-cut butterfly-Amy Butler, journaling pen (EKSuccess Brands); white cardstock (Bazzill); patterned papers (Creative Memories)

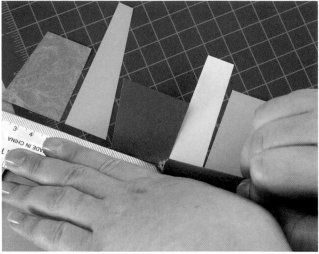

2   With my chipboard frame created, I begin adhering bits and pieces of pattern paper. Make sure that all your scraps have straight edges, and continue lining them up until the frame is completely filled.

3   Once the frame is completely filled, flip it over onto the cutting mat and trim off all the excess paper.

Tips

· · · · · · · · · ·

* *Once finished, it would be very easy to either cut straight lines, waves, or whatever type of border you want. I've used cutting systems rather than craft knives in some cases.*

* *Start saving your scraps together so that you have a good selection of pieces to choose from, and they're easily accessible.*

* *If you're apprehensive about which scraps to combine, start with pieces of paper from the same collection, using the fronts and backs of each sheet. These will look great together and help you get the feel of what kind of scrappy look works for you.*

Swing, Swang, Swung

On this layout, I used the technique to make the circular photo frames that I used to help re-create the motion. While the pictures are all very different, I was able to pull them together using the same mix of papers on all three mats. This layout is a good example of my need to mat, and my love for a bit of whimsy all in one.

Supplies: grid patterned paper (Making Memories); yellow border (Bazzill); patterned papers, journaling paper, banner stickers (Jenni Bowlin); letter stickers-Carolee's Creations (ADORNit)

Hybrid

By my definition, hybrid scrapbooking is simply printing some digital element and using it on your paper project. Digital scrapbooking is wonderful, and there are so many amazing options and techniques out there. That's why I'm so passionate about bringing the two worlds together. It doesn't have to be tricky or hard; you can start simple and add techniques to your repertoire as you progress. Just remember, it's all about having creative fun, and when working in digital, you can always just "undo" and start over.

Soiree Box

Using Microsoft Word or another basic program is a great option for the paper crafter looking to add a little digital but not wanting to learn a new program. Using the same process as in *You Are Invited* (page 69), I used Microsoft Word to insert and layer the banner words you see here. The technique is the same one you see me use with photos on page 33, just with digital elements instead. All image files can be treated the same, which makes it easy and fun to print out funky stuff! Creating a banner in Microsoft Word, then printing it out (and cutting it out in banner shape) is something I've not tried before, but I love it! By playing with a simple known technique, I've come up with something entirely new that I'll want to do again and again.

Supplies: patterned paper, large brads (Pink Paislee); digital words (House of 3); small brads (American Crafts); ink-Smooch (Clearsnap); Stickles (Ranger Ink); foam squares (Scrapbook Adhesives by 3L); Other: box

My Notes

Eager to try Katie Pertiet's technique (page 35) for blending image layers and creating unique effects, I played with a few different materials and looks. I printed out my photo (on photo paper), and I also applied a butterfly digital stamp that I'd used with some other layers onto canvas. I started with a small project so if it didn't turn out, I wouldn't have used a lot of product. I love the result! I can see so many cool ways this could work, and so much potential for my hybrid crafting world.

Supplies: butterfly brush, patterned papers-Katie Pertiet (www.designerdigitals.com); canvas, Distress Ink (Ranger Ink); doily (Martha Stewart); rub-on (Hambly Screen Prints); letter stickers (Cosmo Cricket); flag (The Girls' Paperie); rhinestones (EKSuccess Brands); notebook (Moleskine); photo app (iPhone/Hipstamatic)

You Are Invited

Hybrid doesn't get much simpler than this! I layered my tickets in Microsoft Word and printed them onto cardstock, then I tore them out and layered them onto this card. If you're just getting into combining the worlds of digital and paper, doing something very simple is a great way to warm up.

Supplies: digital tickets (House of 3); brad (The Girls' Paperie); stamp (Tim Holtz); Distress Ink (Ranger Ink); button flower (shopEvalicious. com); letter stickers (My Little Shoebox); ribbon (Making Memories); Other: cardstock, crochet flower

Not only can digital techniques be used in paper projects, but it's also possible for digital scrapbookers to be inspired by paper techniques. Looking at all things scrapbooking as potential material for future projects means that you have a bigger selection and lots of options.

Meanderings

As a child, one of Doris Sander's favorite pastimes was digging through her mom's collection of old photographs and wondering what the people in them would say if they could speak. Her style has a distinctly vintage flair, but truly it's a hodgepodge of fun with a solid foundation. One of the things I admire most about her style is her ability to use products in unexpected ways. From flowers on a boy's layout to using nontraditional products on a holiday page, she makes things work for her, and she has a wonderful sense of style. Her blog is a lovely mix of crafting projects and personal stories, and it is always a lot of fun to read.

Doris lives in Tennessee, and when she's not busy teaching, she's crafting up a storm in the scrapbook industry. She loves that scrapbooking allows her to share her stories and thoughts with her son, family, friends and future generations. When it's time to relax, Doris enjoys reading, preferably while drinking a good bottle of Coca-Cola.

Dots and Dabbers

I love making patterns on my pages to help support the themes I want to convey. Paint can be a really fun way to add both color and texture, and thanks to products like Ranger Ink Paint Dabbers, I can add fun to my pages without even getting out a paint brush! I love working with the Paint Dabbers because the vintage color palette is great for my style. When paired with ¾" (2cm) punched circles, I can create a delightful variety of designs.

MATERIALS

Patterned paper (Core'dinations)

Paint dabbers-Lemon Drops, Malted Milk (Ranger Ink)

¾" (2cm) circle punch

Scotch Scrapbooker's Glue

Other: iridescent glitter, vintage dictionary page, cotton thread

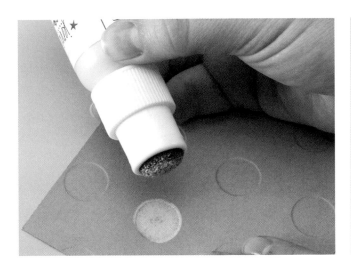

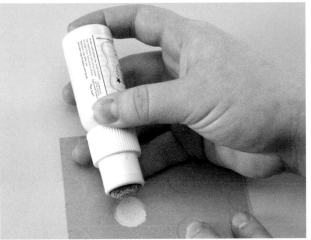

1 To get the paint flowing through the dabber tip, invert the bottle and push the sponge tip against a scrap of paper while gently squeezing the sides. To make a dot, press the sponge tip onto paper and rotate it slightly. Randomly dab some of the cardstock dots with a Lemon Drops Paint Dabber (Ranger Ink).

2 Once the yellow is dry, dab the dots again with a Malted Milk Paint Dabber (Ranger Ink).

« Go!

My favorite technique with the dabber and punched circles combo is the scattered effect onto a dotted design. I often use Core'dinations Large Dot Embossed Cardstock for this, as the size of the dots matches the dabber tip and ¾" (2cm) punch.

Supplies: Paint Dabbers- Lemon Drops, Malted Milk (Ranger Ink); Be Our Guest- Tea Towel, Sewing Room, Home Sweet Home patterned papers, label stickers, buttons, ribbon embellishments, bows, vintage I die-cut journaling card pad (Jenni Bowlin); Ruby Bookprint, Hermitage Large Dot Embossed Cardstock (Core'dinations); Dear Lizzy Puffy Letter Thickers, precision pen (American Crafts); Scrapbooker's Glue (Scotch Brand); Other: vintage dictionary page, cotton thread, iridescent glitter

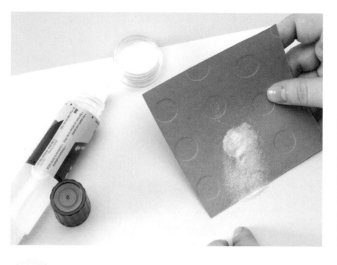

3 Coat each painted dot with Scotch Scrapbooker's Glue and sprinkle with iridescent glitter.

4 Punch circles from a vintage dictionary page and scatter them onto a few of the cardstock dots.

Tips

∗ *Create faux buttons by stitching an X into each center.*

∗ *If you want to use acrylic paint (not in a dabber), use a circle punch to create a mask and paint with a foam brush.*

∗ *This could also be done with mist (and circle punches used as a mask).*

Shine

For this project, I made a fun base for my photo by creating lines of alternating punched paper circles and dabber dots. I then stitched across these lines for a homespun look. To do this, I covered the desired area with lines of dabber dots approximately ¼" (6mm) apart. Then I covered the spaces in between these dots with circles punched from patterned paper and machine stitched across each dotted line.

Supplies: Lemon Drops Paint Dabber (Ranger Ink); Play Date- Naptime patterned paper, mini papers, Family Tree- Aunt Charlotte, mini papers, patterned paper, label stickers, bows, stick pins, mini chipboard butterflies, butterfly banner stickers, butterfly rub-on, alpha minis rub-ons (Jenni Bowlin); embossed cardstock (Core'dinations); seam binding tape (Beaux Regards); letter Thickers, precision pen (American Crafts); Hometown- Main Street patterned paper, Fly a Kite- Dandelions patterned paper (October Afternoon); veneer frames (Studio Calico); Other: vintage dictionary page, rhinestones

Megan Klauer Design MEGAN KLAUER

www.meganklauerdesign.blogspot.com

When I first discovered Megan Klauer's blog, I was blown away by her wonderful work. She's not afraid to play, to get her hands dirty and really go wild with her scrapbooking, and I love that about her. Filled with bright colors, handwritten journaling and amazing photography, her scrapbooking is always inspiring. She fills her blog mostly with scrapbooking projects, sprinkled with lovely photos and glimpses into her everyday life.

Megan calls Illinois home, where she lives with her husband and three children. She scraps for the "me" time, the creative release, and because she loves the patterns, colors and textures. She also loves to blog and connect with the rest of the scrappin' world.

Stamping with Gesso and Mist

This technique is unique because there are so many options with it. Change up the stamp and/or the mist color and it's something completely different!

MATERIALS

Cardstock-white

Gesso

Woodgrain Stamp (Studio Calico)

Mister Huey's Color Mist-Classic Calico (Studio Calico)

Shape punch out/die cut

Other: foam brush, wipe cloth

1 Spread gesso generously onto the cardstock.

2 Immediately press into the gesso with the stamp. Set this aside and allow it to dry fully. The thicker the cardstock or chipboard the better, as the gesso tends to warp the paper otherwise. But make sure it's not too thick if you plan to use a punch.

« Chase @ 5

To me, this technique is the really fun part of the layout. I love this photo of my youngest son, and to pair it with something I created from scratch just makes me happy. The technique allows you to create one-of-a-kind embellishments that can be easily changed up by simply using a different stamp, mist or punch for the final product.

Supplies: cardstock (Bazzill); patterned paper, Mister Huey's Mists, woodgrain stamp (Studio Calico); pattern paper, cardstock letter stickers, chipboard pieces, month paper whimsies (Sassafras Lass); buttons (My Mind's Eye); punches (EKSuccess Brands); adhesive (Xyron); Other: gesso

3 Once the gesso is completely dry, spray with a good amount of mist to saturate the gesso area.

4 Wipe off the extra mist with a paper towel to create a "streaked" effect.

5 At this point, cut out/punch/die cut the stamped cardstock and use it as a unique accent.

Tips

. . . .

✳ *Be sure to wash your stamp as soon as you're finished.*

✳ *Try this technique with acrylic paint, color washes or other mediums for varying looks.*

✳ *Use on the background, to accent near journaling or elsewhere on the page instead of as an accent.*

Love You

Now, take the same technique and apply it to a full 12"x12" (30cmx30cm) piece of pattern paper to create a unique background. I started by applying the gesso randomly on the edges of the page and then repeatedly pressed the stamp in those areas. Top it off with a bit of mist and it creates a fun base to get you started. A great way to use the same woodgrain stamp and technique but in a completely different way!

Supplies: patterned paper, Mister Huey's Color Mist, woodgrain stamp (Studio Calico); patterned paper, cardstock letter stickers, chipboard garden bits, cardstock stickers-flag banners (Sassafras Lass); mini cardstock letter stickers, pattern paper (October Afternoon); cardstock (Bazzill); buttons (My Mind's Eye); resin blooms (Maya Road); corner rounder, label punch (EKSuccess Brands); adhesive (Xyron); Other: gesso

The Moments in Between Lisa Truesdell

www.gluestickgirl.typepad.com

There's a lot to like about Lisa Truesdell (aka the "gluestick girl") and her blog. She mixes stories about her sons with plenty of scrapbook layouts and craft projects. Her layouts are among my favorites. I love how she mixes color, stitching, bits of paper, photos, and always great journaling. She tells her stories, while having fun and playing with paper. What's not to love about that? Her attention to detail, her obsession with Diet Coke from McDonalds, and her daily posts are just a few reasons I enjoy visiting her blog each day.

Lisa lives in Omaha, Nebraska, in a midtown neighborhood filled with big trees and old houses with her husband and sons. When she's not creating pages or chasing her boys, she is slowly teaching herself to use her sewing machine on fabric. She also subscribes to too many magazines and is useless from the moment she starts a new book until she finishes it.

Bubble Boys

I wanted to use paper quilting in a more subtle way on this page. I limited it to two border strips, and used a quieter color scheme. I began by punching circles of patterned paper, and then cutting them in half. I put them back together on a strip of patterned paper, and added stitching. I finished the borders by adding a button to each circle.

Supplies: cardstock (American Crafts); chipboard alphabet (BasicGrey), patterned paper (BasicGrey, My Mind's Eye, Making Memories); orange gems (My Mind's Eye); ink (Jenni Bowlin); paper tape (7gypsies); buttons (Papertrey Ink, Jenni Bowlin); tag (Avery); circle punch (Fiskars); stamp (Studio Calico); pen (STAEDTLER)

Quilted Paper

I love fabric and quilting but don't have the time or skills to really indulge that passion. Instead, I do what I can to bring a similar look to my scrapbook pages. Quilting paper doesn't involve matching up seams or complicated patterns, but it can bring the same cozy feeling to your finished project as a quilt can bring to a room.

MATERIALS

Patterned papers

Cardstock

Other: sewing machine, adhesive, brads, buttons, scissors

1 Search through your scraps of patterned paper and gather ones that match your color scheme. Cut a piece of scrap cardstock to the size you'd like your photo mat to be.

2 Cut your scraps into random rectangles and attach to the scrap cardstock. Don't worry about covering the middle—your photo will hide that part.

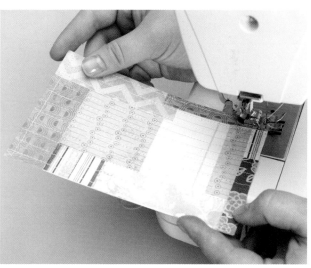

3 Machine stitch vertical lines about ¼" (6mm) apart.

4   Add brads, rub-ons and bits of punched paper to your quilted design.

Tips
......

* *You can keep it monochrome for a calm look, limit it to two or three complementary shades, or make it all-out crazy—whatever fits the look you want!*

* *Use embroidery thread and hand stitch for a different look.*

* *Choose your thread color to add contrast; also, consider zigzag or other decorative stitches to add more interest.*

Bright Eyes

For this page, I wanted to create a photo mat with the look of an old crazy quilt. I gathered patterned papers in shades of blue, yellow and pink and layered together squares of varying sizes. I machine stitched straight lines through the whole mat, and then added my photo. I finished the page by adding extra bits of paper, rub-ons and brads to the mat.

Supplies: blue, yellow script, yellow starburst, apple, pink patterned paper, veneer buttons, veneer letter, green letter stickers, butterfly rub-ons (Studio Calico); blue floral patterned paper (BasicGrey); light blue polka dot patterned paper (Cosmo Cricket); yellow polka dot patterned paper (October Afternoon); ledger patterned paper (Making Memories); pink floral, bright stripe patterned paper (My Mind's Eye); turquoise, yellow patterned paper (Crate Paper); paper tape (7gypsies); tiny attacher (Tim Holtz); yellow mini brads (American Crafts); circle punch (Fiskars); vintage doily punch (Martha Stewart); cardstock (Bazzill); journaling pen (STAEDTLER)

THE MOMENTS IN BETWEEN

Stencil, Scrap and Stitch Title

I love my spray mists and am always looking for new ways to use them. For these pages, I've combined mist with homemade stencils. I love the spray paint effect the overspray brings to the pages—it adds a fun urban edge to the projects. And since I'm making my own stencils, the possibilities for titles and accents are endless.

Silly

I started this page with a layer of light yellow mist on the background and then did the stencil technique over the top with a dark teal. I added brads to each letter to mimic the multicolored polka dot paper, and finished with a small subtitle stitched in place underneath my large stenciled title.

Supplies: mist, ruler (Studio Calico); patterned paper (Studio Calico, We R Memory Keepers, My Mind's Eye); Dear Lizzy- fabric paper (American Crafts); paper doily tape (BasicGrey); ticket (Pink Paislee); letter stickers (Jenni Bowlin); brads (American Crafts); fabric brad (Sassafras Lass); border punch (EKSuccess Brands); font- Reservoir Grunge (Zetafonts); staples (Tim Holtz)

Stencil, Scrap and Stitch Title

MATERIALS

Patterned papers

Cardstock

Letter stickers, spray mist
(Jenni Bowlin)

Other: brads, fabric brad
(Sassafras Lass), paper punch,
craft knife

1 Print your title on scrap cardstock. I find this technique works best with a big, blocky font.

2 Cut out the letters using a craft knife. You'll be discarding the letters and keeping the background paper, so cut carefully!

3 Trim your handmade stencil to the size you want your title block to be. Position your stencil on your background cardstock and spray your mist over it.

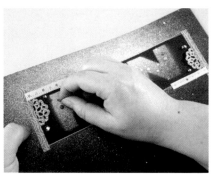

4 Embellish your title block with scraps of paper, buttons and stitching.

Tip

* *When printing on paper for stencils, cardstock will work better than printer paper as a mask as it soaks up less of the mist and is sturdier.*

* *Use a die-cut machine instead of hand cutting.*

* *Reverse by using chipboard or letter stickers as a mask, and tape off a portion of the page for mist as well.*

24 **7** 365

Rather than stencil my title on this page, I opted to use a heart shape to contain my letter sticker title. I added a subtitle, a veneer button and bits of patterned paper and gems to finish off my title block. This variation could also be used repeatedly to create a background for your page.

Supplies: mist, alphabet stickers- yellow, green, veneer buttons, yellow fabric tape, grey, dark blue, letter, ruler patterned paper (Studio Calico); patterned paper, gems (My Mind's Eye); ledger patterned paper (Making Memories); brad (BasicGrey); map patterned paper (October Afternoon)

Iris Babao Uy has been blogging and scrapbooking for quite a few years and her résumé is impressive. What I like most about her is the way she so openly shares her amazing work on her blog. She says that she rarely plans her pages, but rather lets the paper and photos inspire her and goes from there. I'm always blown away by the amount of small embellishments, layers, and amounts of products she's able to work into her pages without making them feel crowded. Somehow, she always manages a great balance, and new blog posts from her are almost always project-filled. I always look forward to them.

Iris lives in the Philippines with her husband and two children. She loves the shabby chic and romantic styles but also enjoys working with bold patterns and striking colors. She has to get it a little messy to consider her page done. If she doesn't have ink and paint on hand, then she's known for tearing little bits of elements and sticking them on randomly for the sheer fun of it.

Sisters

This is a layout featuring a photo of my two daughters. I wanted to add flowers and detail but did not want anything too grand or colorful that would take the focus away from my photo. Using the wire flower technique combined with some cream-colored lace was the perfect solution.

Supplies: papers, lace (Webster's Pages); Say It in Crystals-swirls (Prima Marketing Inc.); stamp (Unity Stamp Co., Stampers Anonymous Stamp); ink- Memento (Tsukineko); mists (Stewart Superior Memories Mist); cardstock, letters (American Crafts)

Wired Flowers

I love lace. I love it so much that I try to find many ways to incorporate it into my pages. Turning lace into wired flowers is one of the things I love to do now.

MATERIALS

Lace flower

Crocheted lace

Copper wire

Round nose pliers

Tulle flower

Tulle fabric

Copper wire

Beads

Craft glue

Lace Flower

1   Take a thin piece of copper wire and thread it on the edge of the lace. Gather the lace and pull the wire to make a tight center. The lace will naturally form a circle.

2   Twist the wire to lock the shape into place.

3   Bend and shape the wire to create the flower center.

Tulle Flower

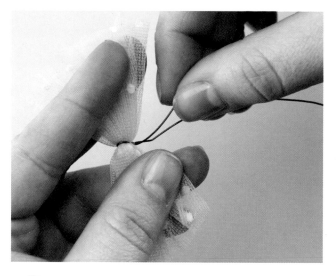

1 Gather a small piece of tulle and secure it in the middle with wire. Twist the wire for added security.

2 Begin threading beads through the wire.

3 Form the beaded wire into a circle.

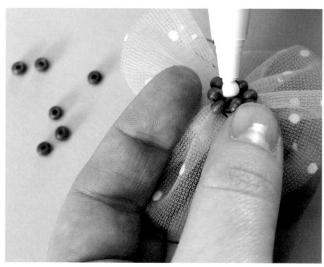

4 Put some craft glue on top of the beads and add more beads on top of the formed circle.

Tips

· · · · · · · · · ·

✻ *Lace, tulle, netting and other materials can be wonderful for this technique.*

✻ *Add beads, small buttons, more wire or otherwise decorate the center.*

✻ *Experiment with different colors and thicknesses of wire.*

This Beauty

In this project, I used tulle and netting instead of lace, and I added beads to the centers. I love how the flowers add both color and whimsical touches to my collage collection of elements on this page. The soft feminine blooms accent my beautiful girl so well—I just love the results!

Supplies: papers, embellishments (Little Yellow Bicycle); chipboard shape, flair buttons (American Crafts); tulle/netting (Webster's Pages); craft envelope (Maya Road); stamp (Stampington & Company); ink-Memento (Tsukineko); mists (Memories Mist)

Over the Rainbow

KESHET SHENKAR STARR

www.keshetstarr.com

Keshet Starr is new to my blog must-reads, but I daresay she is destined to remain a favorite for a long time. She has a playful way with her scrapbook style and an excellent eye for design. I love how she shares her layouts and bits of life with her blog readers in a way that is mostly scrapbook-related. From what she's going to do with vacation photos to recent creations, Keshet is often found sharing on her blog, and I have enjoyed each post from her.

Keshet is a law school graduate living in New Jersey with her husband. She's been scrapbooking for almost ten years and still loves it just as much as the first day she started. When she's not scrapbooking, Keshet enjoys baking, reading novels, creative writing, photography and entertaining.

DIY Layered Embellishments

I love using supplies I have on hand to create my own original embellishments. This saves me money and allows me to mix and match bits and pieces that I adore. With this technique, I'll show you how to use anything from fabric strips and journaling spots to letter stickers and buttons to create your own layered flowers.

MATERIALS

Patterned papers

Cardstock

Paper punches-circle, scallop

Glitter letter stickers

Sticky fabric strips-fabRips
(Studio Calico)

Other: staples, stapler, glue

1 Punch a scallop shape from cardstock and a circle shape out of yellow patterned paper and glue the pieces together.

2 Adhere the letter stickers to the yellow circle.

« I Believe in Pink

On this layout, I used the layered embellishment technique to create a heart-shaped embellishment. I pleated the fabric strip and added a scalloped heart from a punch and a traditional heart shape that I hand cut on top of it. I then layered a paper strip and button to create a finished look. For the rest of the layout, I layered bits and pieces of paper, fabric and rub-ons to create a layered, homespun look.

Supplies: pink floral paper, pink glitter letters (American Crafts); cardstock (Bazzill); scalloped heart punch (EK Success Brands); rub-on (Lily Bee Designs); paper strip (Making Memories); doily punch (Martha Stewart); pink grid paper, gray dot paper (October Afternoon); pleated ribbon (Pink Paislee); yellow fabric (Sandi Henderson Design); blue glitter letters (Sassafras Lass); blue paper (Scarlet Lime); fabRips fabric strip (Studio Calico); pen (Tombow); yellow label (Two Girlz Stuff); Other: button, shipping label

3   Punch a scallop out of spare cardstock and begin pleating the fabric fabRip around the cardstock circle.

4   Complete the pleats around the cardstock circle. Then, staple the pleats of fabRip to the scalloped circle.

5   Attach the gray and yellow scalloped circles to the pleated fabRip to complete the embellishment.

Tips

. . . .

* *Instead of letter stickers, you could decorate the top layer of the embellishment with buttons, journaling spots or an epoxy sticker.*

* *Pleat tissue or crepe paper to get a softer look that is less bulky than fabric.*

* *Size, materials and look can vary greatly and be adjusted to your preferences.*

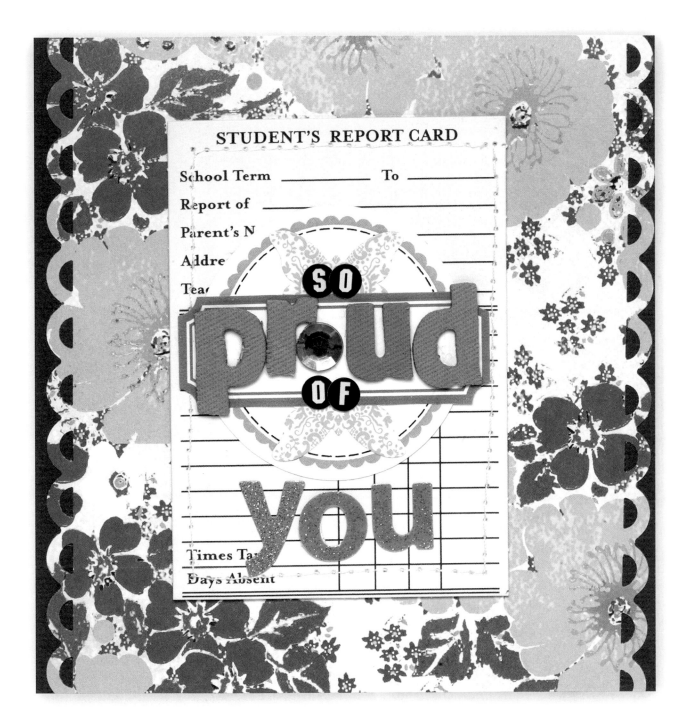

So Proud of You

For this card, I pared down the technique by skipping the fabric strip. Instead, I layered a journaling spot, two butterfly stickers and a label sticker to create an embellishment in the center of the card. Before creating the embellishment, I punched borders onto a piece of patterned paper and adhered it to the card. I sewed a border on a vintage report card and then layered the embellishment on it. I added a title by using large and small letter stickers, as well as a gem in place of a missing letter "o."

Supplies: pink letter stickers (American Crafts); cardstock (Bazzill); scalloped circle journaling spot (Elle's Studio); sewing machine (Janome); black letter stickers, yellow butterflies (Jenni Bowlin); blue gem (My Mind's Eye); report card (October Afternoon); letter stickers (Sassafrass Lass); patterned paper (Scarlet Lime); Other: thread

Quite honestly, I am giddy every time I find a new blog post from Dina Wakley. Her art journaling is always an explosion of words and color and technique, and I wish I put more time and effort into my own painting and art journaling to develop that level of skill. Nearly every day on her blog, she shares art journal entries, paper crafting projects and snippets of her very creative life. It is always a pleasure and inspiration to visit her site. She embraces the successes and failures of her art and has such a positive attitude.

Dina has three boys and lives in Glendale, Arizona. She's a docent at Phoenix Art Museum, which allows her to give tours to school children. She loves to teach classes on artsy scrapbooking, art journaling and mixed-media art. When not creating, she loves to travel, eat good food and hang out with friends.

Dear Carter

I started this tag with the swath of green paint. I journaled right onto the dried paint. I wrote a little message to my son Carter. Next, I added the rest of the elements to the tag. I made sure to write the journaling on the back of the tag so my son can read it. I monoprinted with a large swirl. The stars, scallop and tab at the top of the tag are made from my homemade art papers. I take large sheets of watercolor paper and cover them with lots of acrylic paint and textures. Then I cut the sheets for use on my pages and in my art journal.

Supplies: large manila tag (XpressTags); acrylic paint (Liquitex); Claudine Hellmuth acrylic paint, archival black ink pad (Ranger Ink); water-based poster-paint marker (Sharpie); thread (Gutermann); watercolor paper (Canson); alphabet stamps (Stampin' Up!); Other: vintage dictionary paper

Painted Layers

I love to keep an art journal. My art journals are brightly colored, unstructured and heavily layered. The painted layers technique is a simple way to get an art journal look and feel on your scrapbook pages without a lot of work. You start with a basic painted layer, and then you create your page on top of that layer. When you're finished creating your page, you end up with one more painted layer. The two layers of paint work together to give you that fun, artsy look.

MATERIALS

Large manila tag (XpressTags)

Acrylic paint (Liquitex)

Patterned paper
(Hambly Screen Prints)

Alphabet stickers
(American Crafts)

Claudine Helmuth acrylic paints
(Ranger Ink)

Marker (Sharpie)

Other: palette knife, vintage dictionary paper, thread, sewing machine, black ink, scrap cardstock, letter stickers, paintbrush

1 Select a color of acrylic paint. Use a palette knife to swipe some of the paint onto your tag or cardstock. Don't worry about making it even or exact, just swipe it on and let it dry. This swatch of color becomes your foundation layer; the layer upon which you'll build the rest of the layout.

2 Grab a pen and write some journaling directly onto the painted layer. I like to use water-based poster-paint Sharpies for this, but any permanent pen will work well. Let your journaling spill out, don't worry about making it perfect. Some of what you write will get covered up by subsequent layers, so don't fall too in love with it, either.

3   Add any photographs and patterned paper you wish. You want elements to overlap, so it's fine to cover up parts of your layers. If you make sure that each layer is overlapping or touching another layer, the layers will be unified and you will have a nice flow to your piece.

4   Grab a piece of scratch cardstock. Use a brush and some white acrylic paint to draw a little design onto the cardstock. I tend to like circles and swirls. Take the cardstock and "stamp" the painted design onto your layout. You just created a "monoprint"— one imprint of the paint design. The imprint will be imperfect, and that's the beauty of it. Paint your design on the scrap cardstock again and stamp it on a different part of your page. Do this several times to create a random, textural layer on your page. This final top monoprinted layer is the finishing artsy touch.

Tips
. . . .

* *If you like this look and want to do more, consider investing in artist acrylic paint, rather than bottles of craft paint. The artist acrylics come in jars or tubes and are nice and thick and won't warp your paper.*

* *To wash your paintbrushes: rinse well, then put a few drops of liquid soap in your palm, and swirl the brushes gently until clean. Then rinse and reshape the bristles and let dry.*

Gemini

This scrapbook page straddles the line between scrapbooking and art journaling. It has freestyle journaling and lots of layers and colors. I started with the swath of aqua paint and then added journaling with a white pen. Next, I added patterned paper, then came the photos and lots of little hand-cut hearts. The hearts and large scallop are from my homemade art papers. I used three small circles for my monoprint layer.

Supplies: cardstock (Bazzill); Adirondack Dabber acrylic paint, Claudine Hellmuth acrylic paint, Archival Ink pad- black (Ranger Ink); acrylic paint (Liquitex); watercolor paper (Canson); alphabet (American Crafts); Bingo card, patterned paper (Jenni Bowlin); thread (Gutermann); water-based poster-paint marker (Sharpie); Other: graph paper

www.scrapbook-trends.com

Color, texture and fun are words I'd use to describe Nathalie Kalbach's style and blog. She is a highly skilled crafter who loves to share her knowledge and finished projects. She is an instructor at heart, a fact that shines through on her blog. She loves to interact with her students and shows off her techniques and experiences, while encouraging crafters to add their own creative kick to the projects. In other words, she shares not only stories from her life and projects, but also the inspiration and technique behind them on her blog.

Nathalie Kalbach and her American husband currently live in Hamburg, Germany. Living in the heart of the city in a neighborhood thriving with art and craft, she is inspired by her urban surroundings. Nat loves to design, teach and write—doing all of it wholeheartedly.

Textured Stencil Embellishments and Backgrounds

I love texturized and dimensional elements on my layouts and this easy technique will add all of this and more. You can create custom embellishments and backgrounds by just layering color and stenciled patterns with an artist's medium, such as gesso. The only real requirement here is to play and have fun! There are many possibilities in stepping up this technique and modifying it to suit your needs.

MATERIALS

Cardstock (Core'dinations)

Screen, Glimmer Mist (Tattered Angels)

Gesso (Golden Artist Colors, Inc.)

Other: flat acrylic

1 Take cardstock, chipboard, canvas or other material and cut it into the desired shape. Lay a screen or stencil over the shape and generously pour out some gesso. Hold down the screen with one of your fingers to make sure it lays flat out on the surface. Use a piece of acrylic, or any rigid water-resistant piece (I use hotel room key cards), to spread gesso over the screen and fill in the open areas of the screen. Proceed until everything is spread evenly. Lay aside the acrylic and carefully lift the screen. Let the shape with the gesso pattern dry completely.

2 Spray Glimmer Mist over the piece.

« Contentment

For this layout, I used colors that are reflected in the photo combined with an intricate designed screen to make my embellishments. To keep the colors of my embellishments from overpowering my photo, I chose to keep my background neutral and simply added some mist splotches and stitching to accent the page.

Supplies: cardstock (Core'dinations); gesso (Golden Artist Color, Inc.); vellum paper (Hambly Screen Prints); screen, Glimmer Mist, Glimmer Glam (Tattered Angels); chipboard letters (Heidi Swapp); black acrylic paint marker (Posca); scrapbook adhesives, crafty power tape (Scrapbook Adhesives by 3L); Other: sewing machine, cardboard for the circles

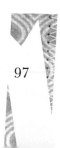

3 Remove any excess liquid.

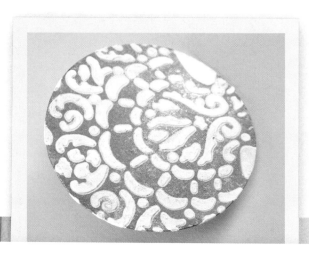

Once complete you will notice a different shade of the color on the gesso part and you can repeat with more colors if desired. The gessoed parts appear much lighter and they take on the sparkles of the mist more, which makes for a wonderful textured and dimensional look.

Tips

* Make sure to wash the screen promptly after use while waiting for the gesso to dry so you do not ruin the screen for future projects.

* The screen or stencil does not have to be the same size as your shape. It can be larger or smaller. In fact, often having the pattern extend past the edges of the shape makes for a more interesting look.

* If you do not have stencils or screens, make your own, use paper punches, or play with texture by spreading the medium and using a plastic knife, needle, fork or other instrument to design your own!

* This technique will also work with multi-medium, molding paste and even acrylic paint.

* In place of mists, feel free to try inks, color washes and other mediums.

* This technique isn't limited to shapes! Use directly on your project, as a background or on title letters.

Childhood

For this canvas, I took the technique up a notch. Instead of a small piece, I did the technique on the entire background. First, I placed the little circles on the canvas and then the screens above. I applied gesso to the whole canvas over the screens and then lifted the screens, as well as the circles. After it dried and I misted the various colors, I used Ranger's Perfect Pearls to add even more dimension and texture by tracing the screen patterns.

Supplies: gesso, gel medium (Golden Artist Color, Inc.); chipboard letters (Heidi Swapp); Glimmer Mist, Chalkboard Glimmer Mist, Glimmer Glaze, Glimmer Glam, screens, stamps (Tattered Angels); Perfect Pearls, Glossy Accents, Archival Ink (Ranger Ink); Crafty Power Tape, foam squares (Scrapbook Adhesives by 3L); Other: canvas, tissue paper, canvas fabric

Scrapperlicious   IRENE TAN   *www.scrapperlicious.blogspot.com*

Irene Tan's work is filled with bold colors, loads of florals and lots of fun. I love tuning into her blog to find the kinds of layouts and projects that you can stare at for a long time. She has so much detail and interesting layers in her work, it's truly a pleasure and always an inspiration. She also shares information and helpful tips on how she created her work, which is always appreciated. Irene loves to experiment with all the wonderful crafting and scrapping products available and comes up with new ideas for using them.

Irene lives with her family in Malaysia, and is known to say, "Scrap with your heart and don't forget to have fun, too!" She is a storyteller and enjoys working with several manufacturers in the scrapbook industry.

Adding Textures and Colors to Clear Acrylic

Acrylic is an interesting element to add to any of your projects. It normally comes in clear, and the transparent effect enables so many possibilities in your creativity. It's that little special touch that I would love to have on most of my projects. This technique offers a way to enhance those acrylic pieces by adding textures and colors. With this technique, you could easily tailor these acrylic pieces to any project you're working with.

MATERIALS

Acrylic butterflies and flowers
(Clear Scraps)

Alcohol Inks (Ranger Ink)

Embossing folder, machine (Sizzix)

Other: paintbrush

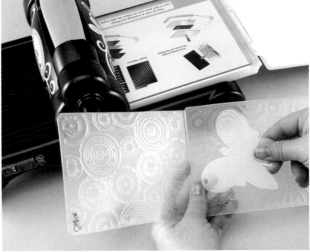

1 Gather an acrylic embellishment or acrylic sheet, an embossing folder (and machine), some alcohol inks and a paintbrush.

2 Line up your piece to emboss on the design that you would like.

« I Love You

For this layout, I embellished acrylic butterflies and flowers. For the butterflies, I embossed and then painted them with various alcohol inks on the back. Then on the front, I rubbed the embossed surfaces with a glue pad and sprinkled some fine glitter over it. I finished by sealing the pieces with dimensional glue. As for the acrylic flower pieces, I also embossed and painted the backs with white acrylic paint. I then colored the embossed images with Copic makers and Zig Painty markers. I also added some glitter glue on its edges and on some of the colored images. Once all of the acrylic embellishing was done, I added the pieces to my layout.

Supplies: acrylic- butterflies, flowers (Clear Scraps); cardstock, pattern papers, chipboard, stickers, flowers, wraps, ribbon (BoBunny Press); cardstock (Bazzill); flowers (Prima Marketing Inc.); Distress Ink, Alcohol Inks, glitter glue, acrylic paint, adhesive (Ranger Ink); glitter (Martha Stewart); markers (Zig); markers (Copic Markers); brads (Karen Foster Design); adhesive (GlueArts); embossing folder, die cuts, machine (Sizzix)

3 Emboss the acrylic using the embossing machine.

4 Your acrylic piece should have a crisp embossing now.

5 Using a paint brush, paint the acrylic embellishment with Alcohol Ink.

6 Layer as many Alcohol Ink colors as you want your adornment to have.

Tips

· · · · · · · · · ·

✳ *To color the acrylics, you could also use Copic markers or acrylic paint.*

✳ *You can apply liquid adhesive on the embossed images and sprinkle some glitters on it for a sparkle effect.*

✳ *Try a similar effect with a transparency or other thin material if acrylic is not available.*

I Adore You Tag

For this project I started with an acrylic tag. Using the embossing folder, I embossed on all four edges of the tag and then inked it with some alcohol ink. This left room for me to add a sentiment and some fun embellishments to add even more layers, and plenty of bold color to my tag.

Supplies: acrylic tag (Clear Scraps); pattern papers, chipboard, stickers, lace, wraps, ribbon, rub-on, brads (BoBunny Press); flowers (Accent Scrapbooking); Distress Inks, Alcohol Inks (Ranger Ink); adhesives (Tombow, GlueArts); embossing folders, machine (Sizzix)

If you're looking for a superhero of all things inked, stamped and funky, then be sure to watch Wendy Vecchi. Her blog is filled with all kinds of projects and innovative ideas for using products that I have, as well as showing me products I might have otherwise not considered. Her vintage-inspired style is eclectic, with an exceptional attention to detail and a fresh approach to the creative spirit. She shares her love of techniques and reminds you that whatever you do each day, just "make art!"

Home for Wendy is Illinois, when she's not on the road teaching. Wendy loves to demo and teach at stores and events across the country, and her work has been featured in numerous publications. Wendy has her own line of stamps titled "Studio 490" as well as a signature "Art Parts" collection available from Stampers Anonymous.

Where Love Resides

I love flowers and houses, so this piece fits the bill. Creating little works of art to be used as home décor is both fun and a great way to test out new possibilities. I used one of my Art Parts (a line I design) homes for this project. I used the masking plaid technique to create a grungeboard flower to embellish the home. I really like layering flowers, and this project is no exception.

Supplies: Manila tag, Ink Blending Tool, Distress Inks- Weathered Wood, Walnut Stain, Forest Moss, Faded Jeans (Ranger Ink); Idea-ology- tissue tape, grungeboard, background paper, heart, long fastener, star stamp (Tim Holtz); Stampers Anonymous- art parts- home, leaves, circle, scallop trim shapes (Studio 490); Studio 490- screen, polka dots, flowers, guaranteed by, home, ticking stamps (Stampers Anonymous)

Life's a Trip ATC

For this project I switched it up and used the technique for the background, instead of for the main embellishment. You can see that this technique has tons of possibilities, by just changing the color of the inks used and varying the placement of the tissue tape strips.

Supplies: Stampers Anonymous: art parts ATC, vintage truck, flower, leaves shapes (Studio 490); Idea-ology- long fasteners, hitch fastener, (Tim Holtz); Distress Inks- Brushed Corduroy, Weathered Wood, Faded Jeans, Forest Moss, Archival Ink- Jet Black, Heirloom Gold Perfect Pearls Mist (Ranger Ink)

Masked Plaid

I'm one to look at all the possibilities and to try to find new things to do with my favorite products. One happy discovery I've made is that tissue tape is wonderful for creating masked plaid. I have done this with inks, color washes and mists, and it's such creative fun! This technique can be done on chipboard, cardstock, manila tags, grungeboard or any other surface you'd like. It's so simple, and once you're finished, you can create anything from a die cut to a custom background.

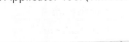

MATERIALS

Tissue tape (Tim Holtz)

Manila tag

Distress Ink-Antique Linen, Stormy Sky, Bundled Sage (Ranger Ink)

Ink Applicator Tool (Tim Holtz)

21
22
23
24
25
26
27
28
29
30
31

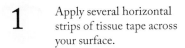

1 Apply several horizontal strips of tissue tape across your surface.

2 Use the blending tool with the ink of your choice (I used Antique Linen Distress Ink) and ink over the entire surface. Then remove the tissue tape strips.

3 Reapply the tissue tape strips, but this time place them vertically. Ink (Stormy Sky Distress Ink) over the entire surface in the same manner, then remove the tape strips.

4 Use the blending tool and ink Bundled Sage Distress Ink over the entire surface.

Tips

....

* *Technique can also be done with mist, color wash or other color medium.*

* *Consider the order in which you're layering colors and how the end result will turn out.*

* *Step it up by stamping an image or pattern, die cutting, punching or otherwise transforming your basic plaid.*

Tammy Tutterow

www.tammytutterow.typepad.com

When I think of Tammy Tutterow and her blog, I picture all things shabby, vintage and distressed. She has a gift for highly intricate projects, but most importantly Tammy is fantastic at sharing her enthusiasm and how-to of her craft. From home decor items to layouts, and every possible project in between, Tammy is gifted in all kinds of crafting. She often refers to herself as a "stuff maker" because she is at her creative happiest when she makes things to decorate her home. Her love of crafting and of sharing her ideas is infectious. It's hard not to love visiting her blog.

Tammy lives with her husband and three children in St. Louis, Missouri. In addition to being a designer and instructor, she works part-time as a 911 dispatcher. She is a fair-weather gardener, so if the spring breezes are blowing, and she's not crafting, you will probably find her playing in the dirt in her flower garden.

Always make time for love.

Crackled Metal Charms

I really love the crackle effect created by Distress Crackle Paint. I tried many times to use it on metal surfaces, only to have it peel and flake off. I was determined to make it work, so I experimented until I discovered a solution. By layering it with Glossy Accents, Distress Crackle Paint will not only stay put, it will meld with the Glossy Accents to create a crackled and crazed finish that is smooth to the touch with no flaking! This technique works great to add a unique finish to metal embellishments that are smooth or embossed.

MATERIALS

Alcohol Ink-assorted colors, Archival Ink-Jet Black, Glossy Accents, Distress Crackle Paint-Clear Rock Candy, Ink Applicator Tool with felt pads (Ranger Ink)

Metal charm

Other: foam brush

1 Apply a selection of Alcohol Ink colors to the felt of an Ink Applicator Tool.

2 Tap the ink onto a metal charm with a raised embossed design. Continue applying layers of color until you obtain a look that you like.

« Make **Time** Photo Frame

I love to make embellished photo frames from frames I find on the clearance aisle of my local arts and crafts store. They are often scratched and damaged. Since I re-cover the frames with scrapbook paper, the damage doesn't matter much to me. For this frame, I began by re-covering the front of it with dictionary print scrapbook paper. The paper features several inspiring words, including the word "time." I decided to use time as a focus for my frame. After covering the frame, I embellished it with a cluster of flowers and used a watch face finished with the crackled metal technique as a focal point.

Supplies: Idea-ology- paper, time piece, game spinners, stickers, Stampers Anonymous- Floral Tattoo Stamp Set (Tim Holtz); Chantilly Collection Velvet Hydrangeas (Petaloo); Alcohol Inks, Archival Ink pad, Ink Applicator Tool with felt pads, Glossy Accents, Stickles-Star Dust, Distress Crackle Paint- Clear Rock Candy, Distress Ink-Vintage Photo (Ranger Ink); Multi Medium Matte-decoupage (Claudine Hellmuth Studio); cardstock stickers (BasicGrey); 3D Foam Squares (Therm O Web); 450 Quick Dry (Helmar USA Inc.); Other: wood photo frame, sewing machine

3   Use an Archival Ink pad to brush over the surface of the design. Applying ink on the raised portions of the design will accent them and help them stand out.

4   Use a foam brush to apply Glossy Accents to the surface of the charm. Apply a smooth level, making sure to cover the piece completely in all nooks and grooves of the design. You may get bubbles from the foam brush as you dab the Glossy Accents into any grooves. You may either brush them out or leave them as is; most will disappear as the Glossy Accents dry. Set the piece aside to dry for at least one hour.

5   Once the Glossy Accents is thoroughly dry, brush on a layer of Rock Candy Distress Crackle Paint.

Tip

Allow the Distress Crackle Paint to dry completely. Once dry, the surface of the charm will look crackled and crazed but be smooth to the touch and will not flake off. You can create your own charms easily by embossing thin pieces of metal in embossing folders in a die cut machine. If you plan to use the piece as wearable art, be sure to smooth or fold in any sharp edges.

Life is either a daring adventure or nothing. To keep our faces toward change and behave like free spirits in the presence of fate is strength undefeatable.
*Helen Keller

Butterfly Greeting Card

The crackled metal technique not only makes a great embellishment for a papercraft project, it also can be used for wearable art jewelry pieces. The crackled metal technique is perfect for adding color and texture to purchased embossed brass charms and is durable enough to be worn. For this example, I added a simple jewelry pinback to the back of a purchased charm that was embellished using the crackled metal technique. To make the pin presentable for gift giving, I embellished a plain card front with a piece of scrapbook paper, some stamping and flowers. I punched a set of holes in the card front so that I could insert the pin onto the card for display. The pin then doubles as an embellishment and a gift.

Supplies: Idea-ology- paper, Stampers Anonymous-Floral Tattoo Stamp Set (Tim Holtz); Chantilly Collection Velvet Hydrangeas (Petaloo); Butterfly Grandeur metal charm (Vintaj Natural Brass Co.); Alcohol Ink, Archival Ink-Jet Black, Ink Applicator Tool with felt pads, Glossy Accents, Stickles- Star dust, Distress Crackle Paint- Clear Rock Candy, Distress Ink- Vintage Photo (Ranger Ink); Basics Labels Cardstock Stickers (BasicGrey); Memory Tape Runner XL, E-6000 (Therm O Web); Other: foam brush, card/envelope, jewelry pinback, sewing machine

TAMMY TUTTEROW

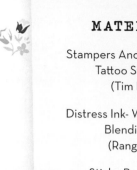

MATERIALS

Stampers Anonymous Floral Tattoo Stamp Set
(Tim Holtz)

Distress Ink- Wild Honey, Ink Blending Tool
(Ranger Ink)

Sticky-Back Canvas
(Claudine Hellmuth Studio)

Single Color Ink Patterned Canvas

I really love creating my own colored and patterned fabric for projects using Sticky-Back Canvas, Distress Inks and stamps. I especially love that this technique uses just one color of ink to create a monochromatic pattern that gives the effect of multiple shades of the same color. Using inks and stamps to create backgrounds on neutral colored materials, like canvas and cardstock, means that I always have the tools on hand to create a background or accent tailored to match my project perfectly.

Supplies: cardstock (Bazzill); Stampers Anonymous Floral Tattoo Stamp Set, Idea-ology Foliage (Tim Holtz); Mini Mono Stickers (BasicGrey); Distress Ink Wild Honey, Vintage Photo, Ink Blending Tool (Ranger Ink); manila ledger paper; Thickers Salutations Fabric Letter Stickers (American Crafts); Mulberry Wild Roses- gold (Petaloo); gold ribbon (Hanah Silk Ribbon); Memory Tape Runner XL (Therm O Web); Other: sewing machine

Nature's Gold

When I sat down to create a scrapbook page featuring photos from my garden, I decided I wanted to create a color-based page that would draw attention to the gold and yellow colors of the page. I had the perfect colored alphabet stickers on hand but no background paper to match. I used the same inking and stamping from my canvas project, but used textured cardstock in place of the canvas to create a background paper that not only matched my letter stickers but also added to the theme I was creating. The stamped ink accented the texture of the cardstock adding visual interest to the background while still staying neutral enough to allow the photos to be the focus.

1 Apply the desired color of Distress Ink to a piece of Sticky-Back Canvas using an Ink Blending Tool. Begin applying the ink at the outer edges, working in a circular motion onto your canvas. Continue applying the ink to the canvas until it is covered with color.

2 Ink a stamp with the same color of Distress Ink and begin stamping randomly on the canvas. Once the ink is dry, use the piece in your project as desired.

Believe Photo Frame

Sticky-Back Canvas is a great product for home decor projects. Because it already has adhesive applied to the back of it and because the fabric is very pliable, it can be used to easily cover shaped projects like photo frames. For this frame, I created a color and pattern on my piece of canvas that matched the decor of the room I planned to display the frame in. By creating my own background, I was able to create a pattern that was interesting but not overpowering or distracting from the photo in the frame.

Supplies: Sticky-Back Canvas (Claudine Hellmuth Studio); Stampers Anonymous Floral Tattoo Stamp Set, Idea-ology Memo Pin, Corners, Philosophy tags (Tim Holtz); Distress Ink- Wild Honey, Vintage Photo, Ink Blending Tool (Ranger Ink); Mulberry Wild Roses- gold (Petaloo); Galaxy Stars, Calcutta Leaves (Prima Marketing Inc.); gold ribbon (Hanah Silk Ribbon); Adhesive-450 Quick Dry (Helmar USA, Inc.); Other: velvet trim

Tips

. . . .

* *The finished canvas piece not only looks nice but also adds an element of texture to any project. It can be used for a variety of different projects, such as scrapbook pages, cards, tags, mini books and home decor pieces.*

* *As an alternative to canvas, try using textured cardstock. The finished effect is very similar and is a less expensive alternative.*

111

The Scrappy Jedi MELISSA L. STINSON *www.scrappyjedi.com*

I first discovered Melissa Stinson's blog during an online class I was teaching (and she was taking). She is so completely herself—so clearly a woman who knows what she likes and isn't afraid of being a science-fiction loving geek. I just loved her to pieces for it. Not being much of a *Star Wars* fan myself, I don't always share her enthusiasm, but her gift for writing and storytelling, and her awesome talent in scrapbooking, keep me coming back for more. She shares favorite crafty things from around the Web, her own creations, talks about products and her process, and so much more. A girl after my own heart, she's been known to stash chocolate in several hiding places around her scrap space.

Melissa has been scrapbooking for almost thirteen years. Her parents gave her a camera as a high school graduation gift, and soon after she found herself in the paper aisle at a local craft store and has been hooked ever since. She is a self-proclaimed "geek girl" who loves science-fiction and works full-time as an engineer, but who also spends her nights and weekends on more crafty endeavors.

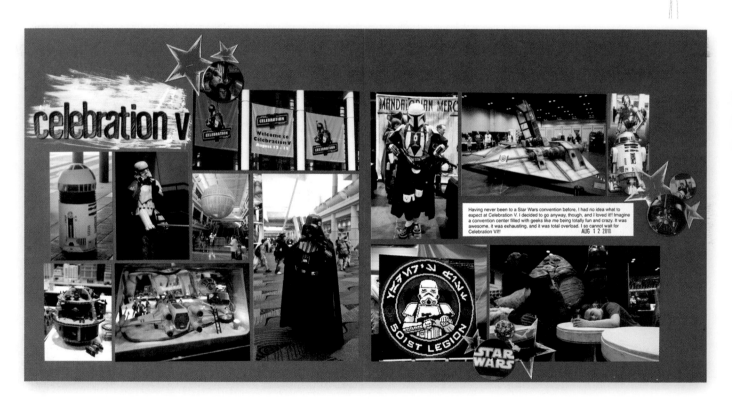

Celebration V

I love that the buttons on this layout were made using an advertisement for lunchboxes that I picked up on the convention show floor. I used my circle dies to cut out only the characters and logos in the ad and created a set of embellishments that I simply could not have purchased anywhere!

Supplies: cardstock (Bazzill); transparent stars (Heidi Swapp/Advantus); staples (Tim Holtz/Advantus) letter stickers (American Crafts) paint (Making Memories)

Custom Chipboard Buttons

Sometimes it can be difficult to find the perfect embellishment for your layout, even with the multitude of ready-made options available. In these cases, making your own embellishments is a fun and creative alternative to purchasing and can lead to accents that you could never find in any store!

Chipboard buttons are a popular embellishment and are commercially available in a variety of themes, but they're also very simple to make yourself. Chances are that you already have everything you need on hand! They're also a great option for including "life stuff" on your layouts—all those little bits and pieces that you collect from events and travels but may struggle (as I do) to use on your layouts.

MATERIALS

Patterned paper

Adhesive sheets

Chipboard

Circle die cut, circle punch, scissors or craft knife

Craft hammer

Manual punch

1 Cover the back of your patterned paper with adhesive. Xyron, Mod Podge or adhesive sheets are ideal, but any adhesive will do as long as you completely cover the back of your paper.

2 Adhere patterned paper to chipboard. The thickness of the chipboard will depend on the depth of the die/punch you are using (I've found that the chipboard from the backs of paper stacks are perfect). Grungeboard is also a great option as a base.

3 Place a circle die over the portion of the patterned paper you want to use as your button, then run it through your die-cutting machine according to the manufacturer's directions. If you don't have a die-cutting machine, then several punched or hand-cut cardstock circles can be stacked and adhered together to simulate chipboard, then topped with a punched piece of patterned paper.

4 Mark the areas to be punched out to make the button's holes using a pen or paper piercer. I find it helpful to use another button as a guide for hole placement, especially when making buttons with four holes.

5 Punch out the button's holes a Crop-A-Dile, heavy-duty paper punch, or a manual punch (pictured) are all good options. Keep the holes relatively small.

6 Coat the button with a clear dimensional adhesive such as Diamond Glaze or Glossy Accents (UTEE or a matte finish adhesive area also great alternatives). If you're using a liquid adhesive, start by making a ring around the outside of the button to ensure coverage all the way to the edge, then fill in the interior.

Tips

* *Skip the dimensional adhesive and let your patterned paper retain its original finish.*

* *Instead of patterned paper, use memorabilia, magazine pages, maps, ephemera, ticket stubs, pieces of your child's artwork or vintage book pages.*

* *Coat the top of your chipboard button with a layer of glitter, Stickles or paint.*

* *Cover your buttons with fabric or Sticky-Back Canvas.*

* *Cut your buttons into shapes other than circles. Stars, butterflies and shells are just a few ideas.*

* *Skip punching holes in your buttons to make custom accents.*

114

Darren and I escaped the cold weather at home to spend a few days before Christmas reading, relaxing, and exploring in the Bahamas.

December 16-21, 2010

The Nassau Before Christmas

The buttons on this layout have been coated in a thick layer of glitter glue and used as flower centers. Chipboard buttons are as versatile as any conventional button and can be used in countless ways.

Supplies: cardstock (Bazzill); tropical flowers, pearls, turquoise paper flower (Prima Marketing Inc.); patterned paper, other paper flowers, buttons, leaves (Making Memories); large letter stickers (American Crafts); small letter stickers (My Little Shoebox); glitter glue (Ranger Ink)

Traveling at the Speed of Life KENDRA MCCRACKEN

www.kendramccracken.blogspot.com

Kendra McCracken's blog, like her crafting style, is homespun, full of vivid detail and always a lot of fun. Whether she's posting about something her sons have done, sharing a new project or showing images from inside her beautiful studio, Kendra has a gift for sharing and an enjoyable reading style. I always find myself both overwhelmed by her talent and utterly inspired by all that she manages to do with such simple supplies. Most of her projects involve mixed media—from fabrics and stitching, to papers and punching—you'll always get a vintage-inspired work of art. Although, you can never anticipate exactly what Kendra will do with the supplies on hand.

Kendra lives in the Missouri countryside with her husband and sons. Her favorite color combination is red, turquoise and cream, and you'll find it frequently in her projects. She blogs from her desk that sits by a window looking out over her garden and a pasture, and she enjoys every minute.

Vintage-Inspired Fabric Letters

I adore fabric and use it on nearly everything I create. Sometimes it's just a little scrap that I see lying in my creative mess that has frayed in a way that looks pretty to me. Sometimes it's intentional and planned as a focal point from the very beginning. The latter is the case with this project.

My son laughs at me when we're shopping together and I stop to closely examine the details on articles of clothing. He knows I look at everything with inspirational eyes and whatever I'm looking at will end up on a scrapbook layout or craft project. The inspiration for these fabric numbers is the vintage look of the frayed and stitched lettering that I have seen on American Eagle hoodies.

MATERIALS

Chipboard numbers

Fabric: the focal and the heavy-weight background fabric

Lightweight fusible web

Other: pen, scissors, embroidery floss, needle, iron

1 Iron lightweight fusible web to the back side of the focal fabric and transfer the lettering (in reverse format) to the paper covering of the fusible web.

2 Cut out the letters and iron them onto a soft background fabric that is woven from a larger fiber. This will give a softer, thicker look to your frayed edges.

« Since 1922

My grandfather died a few weeks ago and I wanted to do a scrapbook layout about his impact on the people who crossed his path throughout his life. He was born in 1922 and I thought this would be the perfect opportunity to use this vintage-inspired fabric lettering technique.

Supplies: cardstock (Bazzill); patterned paper (Sassafras Lass, October Afternoon); letter stickers, journaling card (Jenni Bowlin); gaffer tape (7gypsies); letter rub-ons (American Crafts); brads (BoBunny Press); star punch (Fiskars); Other: fabric, crocheted trim, wooden bird, embroidery floss

3   Cut a large square around the letter (*Note: This will make the piece more manageable while stitching. It will be cut down further later.)* and hand or machine stitch around the perimeter of the letters. I kept this project simple but any amount of decorative stitching can be added to the centers of the letters.

4   Cut around the outer edge of the letters, leaving about a ⅛" (3mm) border and fray the border with your fingers.

Tips

* *A loose or larger fiber material will be easier to fray as your background.*

* *Contrast between fabrics used and your thread of choice can help create a very bold, to a very subtle look.*

* *Depending on patterns and fabrics chosen, this technique can work for anything from shabby vintage to grungy urban!*

* *Beyond letters, this technique will work on shapes or to create a matting element for your crafting project.*

* *You'll find fusible web in fabric craft stores in packages or on bolts. You can purchase the smallest amount the store will cut (usually ⅛ yard) for this project.*

* *Burlap is a great fabric to use for a warm, grungy look to add to your letters and layouts.*

Happy Birthday Card

This technique can be used for shapes, as well as numbers and letters. In this example, you can see how I've used it on a heart and a circle, as well as added textured bits and pieces in the form of a banner and strips to create a memorable birthday card.

Supplies: cardstock (Bazzill); brad (BoBunny Press); Other: fabric, crochet thread, crocheted trim, embroidery floss

Messy

Some scrapbookers embrace it, others avoid it and some are fearful of it. I'm talking about the messy stuff. Paints, gesso, mists, inks, glitters and everything in between—it's the side of scrapbooking that ventures into mixed media and definitely messy territory.

I have advice if you're just getting into this stuff. Getting a big box or tub to work in for mists and anything that has spray to it is good (so you don't spray your house up!). Also, baby wipes are excellent hand and surface cleaners, and be sure to wipe off and clean any tools and surfaces immediately before paints or other mediums dry.

We have covered a lot of wonderful "messy" materials in this book, and I'd like to share a few projects with you that I created based on those techniques and supplies:

The Best Sister

The inspiration here came straight from Lisa Dickinson (page 49) and her use of stencils on layouts. I outlined the template (it took less time than I would have thought) and misted it, then added Stickles, paints and even cut a few out to add more fun and depth to it—wow. For the title, I outlined my letter stickers, then painted over the area with crackle paint and removed the letter sticker. The result? Another fun masked layer on top of the stars. Such big messy fun, and a great way to use random letter stickers that aren't the right color.

Supplies: star template (The Crafter's Workshop); patterned papers (Pink Paislee); letter stickers (Doodlebug); Distress Stickles, Crackle Paint, white enamel accents (Ranger Ink); mist (Tattered Angels); small block letter stickers (The Girls' Paperie)

Fly

I started this tag by trying Kelly Purkey's technique (page 53) for embossing and misting, but the image and colors I used didn't show up well. Determined just to play and have a good time, I was going to try Dina Wakley's journaling technique (page 93) but then I changed my mind and stamped onto it instead. At that point, I just started adding, playing and enjoying the time with my messiest of supplies.

That is really the key with this stuff: Just play around, get comfortable and have fun. Sometimes experiments turn into cool new ideas, and the more you sit back and enjoy, the better time you're going to have and the more likely you'll be to like the results, as well.

Supplies: wood butterflies, rub-on butterflies, patterned paper, mist, cloud stamp (Studio Calico); beads (Making Memories); trim (Webster's Pages); fly stamp (Catslife Press); Distress Stickles, Crackle Paint, Glossy Accents (Ranger Ink)

Some tips for playing with messy stuff—remember that often you can substitute out mediums. Instead of ink, you can paint on a color wash or mist. Don't have mists? Water down some paint or work with distress ink that can be used with water. If trying to create a resist embossing powder, multi-medium, some sealants and products like Glossy Accents (Ranger Ink) can all work in place of one another.

Finally, the artists in this book who specialize in this messy stuff are wonderful teachers. Often, on their blogs, I find inspiration, tutorials, videos and more.

Teacher Card

Nathalie Kalbach showed off some really incredible ways to get textured accents (page 97), but I decided I wanted to try her idea in a different way—with patterned papers and using multi-medium as a resist surface. This made an incredible mess, but I love the results so much! I simply held down my stencil, applied the multi-medium, then removed the stencil and washed it away. Once dry, I misted the surface and wiped away the excess. I did this on a paper-covered chipboard apple, as well as used an owl stencil over patterned paper that I then cut out and applied to my apple. These two pieces went so well together, and I felt like it made such a great teacher card—I went for it. I love it when messy play and experiments work themselves into useful little projects.

Supplies: Damask template (The Crafter's Workshop); owl template, glimmer mist (Tattered Angels); red star patterned paper (Pink Paislee); text patterned paper (The Girls' Paperie); multi-medium (Claudine Hellmuth Studio); letter stickers (Glitz Designs); chipboard apple (Maya Road); Distress Ink, white enamel accents (Ranger Ink); Other: cardstock

121

Source Guide

The following companies manufacture products featured in this book. Please check your local retailers to find these materials, or go to a company's website for the latest product. In addition, we have made every attempt to properly credit the items mentioned in this book. We apologize for any company that we have listed incorrectly, and we would appreciate hearing from you.

7gypsies
www.sevengypsies.com

Accent Scrapbooking
www.accentscrapbooking.com

Adobe
www.adobe.com

ADORNit
www.adornit.com

Advantus
shopadvantus.com

American Crafts
www.americancrafts.com

Anna Griffin
www.annagriffin.com

BasicGrey
www.basicgrey.com

Bazzill
www.bazzillbasics.com

BIC
www.bicworld.com

BoBunny Press
www.bobunny.com

Catslife Press
www.catslifepress.com

Cavallini Papers & Co., Inc.
www.cavallini.com

Claudine Hellmuth Studio
www.claudinehellmuth.com

Clear Scraps
www.clearscraps.com

Clearsnap
www.clearsnap.com

Core'dinations
www.coredinations.com

Cosmo Cricket
www.cosmocricket.com

The Crafter's Workshop
www.thecraftersworkshop.com

Crate Paper
www.cratepaper.com

Creative Charms
www.creativecharms.com

Creative Imaginations
www.creativeimaginations.us

Creative Memories
www.creativememories.com

DesignerDigitals
www.designerdigitals.com

Divine Twine
whiskergraphics.com

DMC
www.dmc-usa.com

Doodlebug Design Inc.
www.doodlebug.ws

Echo Park
www.echoparkpaper.com

Educational Insights
www.educationalinsights.com

EKSuccess Brands
www.eksuccess.com

Elle's Studio
www.shopellesstudio.com

Etsy
www.etsy.com

Fiskars
www.fiskars.com

The Girls' Paperie
www.thegirlspaperie.com

Glitz Design
www.glitzitnow.com

GlueArts
www.gluearts.com

Golden Artist Colors, Inc.
www.goldenpaints.com

Gutermann Thread
www.gutermann-thread.com

Hambly Screen Prints
www.hamblyscreenprints.com

Hanah Silk Ribbon
www.hanahsilkribbon.com

Heidi Swapp
www.heidiswapp.com

Helmar USA, Inc.
www.helmarusa.typepad.com

Hero Arts
www.heroarts.com

House of 3
www.houseof3.com

Imaginisce
www.imaginisce.com

Janome
janome.com

Jenni Bowlin
www.jbsmercantile.com

Karen Foster Design
karenfosterdesign.com

KI Memories
www.kimemories.com

Lily Bee Designs
www.lilybeedesigns.com

Liquitex
www.liquitex.com

Little Yellow Bicycle
www.mylyb.com

Making Memories
www.makingmemories.com

Martha Stewart
www.marthastewart.com

Marvy
www.marvy.com

May Arts
www.mayarts.com

Maya Road
www.mayaroad.com

Microsoft
www.microsoft.com

Moleskine
www.moleskine.com

My Little Shoebox
www.mylittleshoebox.com

My Mind's Eye
www.mymindseye.com

Nikki Sivils Scrapbooker
www.nikkisivils.com

October Afternoon
octoberafternoon.com

Paper Source
www.paper-source.com

Papertrey Ink
www.papertreyink.com

Petaloo
petaloo.cameoez.com

Pink Paislee
www.pinkpaislee.com

Prima Marketing Inc.
www.primamarketinginc.com

Ranger Ink
www.rangerink.com

Rubber Stamp Concepts
www.rubberstampingdepot.com

Sakura
www.sakuraofamerica.com

Sandi Henderson Design
www.sandihendersondesign.com

Sassafras Lass
www.sassafraslass.com

Scarlet Lime
www.scarletlime.com

Scotch Brand
www.scotchbrand.com

Scrapbook Adhesives by 3L
www.scrapbook-adhesives.com

Sharpie
www.sharpie.com

shopEvalicious.com
www.shopevalicious.com

Sizzix
www.sizzix.com

Spellbinders Paper Arts
www.spellbinderspaperarts.com

STAEDTLER
www.staedtler.com

Stampin' Up!
www.stampinup.com

Stampington & Company
www.stampington.com

Stewart Superior-Memories Mist
www.stewartsuperior.com

Studio Calico
www.studiocalico.com

Stampers Anonymous
www.stampersanonymous.com

Sulyn Industries
www.sulyn.com

Therm O Web
www.thermoweb.com

Tim Holtz
www.timholtz.com

Tattered Angels
www.mytatteredangels.com

Tombow
www.tombowusa.com

Tonic Studios
www.tonic-studios.com

Tsukineko
www.tsukineko.com

Uni-ball
www.uniball-na.com

Unity Stamp Co.
www.unitystampco.com

Vintaj Natural Brass Co.
www.vintaj.com

We R Memory Keepers
www.weronthenet.com

Webster's Pages
www.websterspages.com

WorldWin Papers
www.worldwinpapers.com

XpressTags
www.xpresstags.com

Xyron
www.xyron.com

Zetafonts
www.zetafonts.com

Index

Thank you all

A special thanks to all our contributors for sharing their beautiful work and wonderful techniques. Please make sure to visit their blogs to check out more of their work!

Anna Aspnes
www.annaaspnes.typepad.com

Julie Fei-Fan Balzer
www.balzerdesigns.typepad.com

Kimberly Crawford
www.kimberly-crawford.blogspot.com

Lisa Dickinson
www.lisadickinson.typepad.com

May Flaum
www.mayflaum.com

Nora Griffin
www.noragriffin.typepad.com

Debbie Hodge
www.debbiehodge.com

Sasha Holloway
http://sassysasha.typepad.com

Nathalie Kalbach
www.scrapbook-trends.com

Megan Klauer
www.meganklauerdesign.blogspot.com

Kendra McCracken
www.kendramccracken.blogspot.com

Becky Olsen
www.lifeasathreeleggeddog.blogspot.com

Katie Pertiet
www.katiepertiet.typepad.com

Kelly Purkey
www.kellypurkey.typepad.com

Debee Ruiz
www.debeecampos.blogspot.com

Doris Sander
www.sanderdk.typepad.com

Keshet Shenkar Starr
www.kesheststarr.com

Melissa Stinson
www.scrappyjedi.com

Irene Tan
www.scrapperlicious.blogspot.com

Sharyn Tormanen
www.sharyntormanen.typepad.com

Lisa Truesdell
www.gluestickgirl.typepad.com

Tammy Tutterow
www.tammytutterow.typepad.com

Iris Babao Uy
www.irisbabaouy.typepad.com

Wendy Vecchi
www.studio490art.blogspot.com

Dina Wakley
www.dinastamps.typepad.com

Deena Ziegler
www.deenaziegler.typepad.com

15 14 13 12 11   5 4 3 2 1

DISTRIBUTED IN CANADA BY FRASER DIRECT
100 Armstrong Avenue
Georgetown, ON, Canada L7G 5S4
Tel: (905) 877-4411

DISTRIBUTED IN THE U.K. AND EUROPE BY F&W MEDIA INTERNATIONAL
Brunel House, Newton Abbot, Devon, TQ12 4PU, England
Tel: (+44) 1626 323200, Fax: (+44) 1626 323319
Email: enquiries@fwmedia.com

DISTRIBUTED IN AUSTRALIA BY CAPRICORN LINK
P.O. Box 704, S. Windsor NSW, 2756 Australia
Tel: (02) 4577-3555

SRN: W1597
ISBN-13: 978-1-59963-278-0
ISBN-10: 1-59963-278-0

Edited by Bethany Anderson
Designed by Marissa Bowers
Production coordinated by Greg Nock
Photography by Christine Polomsky and Al Parrish

Adobe and Adobe Photoshop are either registered trademarks or trademarks of Adobe Systems Incorporated in the United States and/or other countries.

fw media
www.fwmedia.com

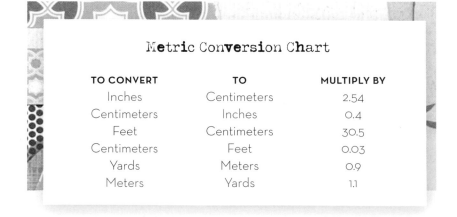

Metric Conversion Chart

TO CONVERT	TO	MULTIPLY BY
Inches	Centimeters	2.54
Centimeters	Inches	0.4
Feet	Centimeters	30.5
Centimeters	Feet	0.03
Yards	Meters	0.9
Meters	Yards	1.1

May

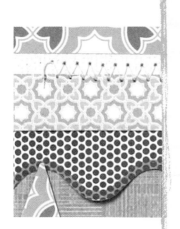

A lifelong crafter, May has been working in the scrapbook industry since 2003. In addition to being an author and published designer, she has taught classes across the United States and online at Big Picture Classes for several years. She has worked with many top manufacturers, including Tim Holtz and Scrapbook Adhesives, and is a contributing writer for Scrapbook Update (an online industry blog). May is the co-author of the Memory Maker's book *Paper+Pixels* and has been blogging since 2005.

Outside of her studio, she is a mother, firefighter's wife, set on auto-mode photographer, avid reader, animal lover and all-around happy woman. She lives in Northern California and tries to find the bright spots in each day. When she's not at the gym or chasing her two daughters around, you will likely find her breaking rules and having a good time in her studio.

Looking for more scrapbook inspiration?

Five reasons to visit
www.memorymakersmagazine.com

* Download FREE projects
* Get expert advice
* Connect with tother scrappers
* Sign up for weekly e-inspiration
* Find the latest news, inspiration, tips and ideas

Shop.MemoryMakersMagazine.com

twitter @fwcraft

facebook @fwcraft

These and other fine Memory Maker titles are available at your local craft retailer, bookstore or online supplier, or visit our website at shop. memorymakersmagazine.com

By Sherry Stevenson

Still looking for that added touch? Embellishments are a quick and fantastic way to quickly add the pizazz to your scrapbook piece or papercraft, and this book covers them all. From rub-ons to eyelets and brads, this really is the handbook for every scrapper.

By Lisa M. Pace

Whether you are a paper crafter or if you are more interested in mixed media, Lisa shares over 40 techniques that can be used on virtually any medium. With her final touches of adding fabric, using molding paste, or being creative with simple paper this book really is for everyone.